THREE SIMPLE TRUTHS

THREE SIMPLE
truths

experiencing them in our lives

adolf hansen

INKWATER
PRESS

PORTLAND • OREGON
INKWATERPRESS.COM

*Scan this QR Code to
learn more about this
title and the author.*

Publisher: Inkwater Press | www.inkwaterpress.com

Paperback ISBN-13 978-1-62901-003-8 | ISBN-10 1-62901-003-0
Kindle ISBN-13 978-1-62901-004-5 | ISBN-10 1-62901-004-9

Printed in the U.S.A.
All paper is acid free and meets all ANSI standards for archival quality paper.

1 3 5 7 9 10 8 6 4 2

DEDICATED

to

NAOMI METZGER HANSEN

my beloved wife

from whom I have received trust

without reservation

and

to whom I have extended trust

without reservation

ever since we met

during our college years

TABLE OF CONTENTS

Preface.. ix

Introduction: Discerning These Truths 1

Chapter 1: God Is Good, All the Time 7

    Character of God 9

    Understanding It 22

Chapter 2: God Works for Good, In Everything 27

    Activity of God... 29

    Participating in It 47

Chapter 3: Trust God, No Matter What...................................51

    Invitation of God 53

    Responding to It.. 66

Postscript: Experiencing These Truths.................................71

Addendum 81

Preface

THREE SIMPLE TRUTHS
That Will Enrich and Sustain Life

Three simple "truths" have the power to enrich and sustain life—regardless of what happens. Each is stated in words we can readily understand. Or so it seems. But when we explore them in greater and greater depth, they become more and more profound.

I've spent a number of years sorting through my beliefs, selecting the three truths that I am convinced are most important, and formulating them into short sentences that anyone can learn and recite. They are:

- God is good, all the time.
- God works for good, in everything.
- Trust God, no matter what.

Other persons share my belief in the significance of these truths and have used them in a variety of settings. The first one has been utilized in many places in a responsive manner; the second has rarely been expressed; the third has been employed in limited contexts. However, these statements have never been considered collectively.

The three truths contain only 17 words: six in the first, six in the second, and five in the third (since the subject is implied). Not only can we easily memorize and recite them, we can also sing or hum them to selected folk tunes. And anyone, of any age, can express them.

The idea of stating the truths in a limited number of words came to me when I remembered how the world-renowned theologian, Karl Barth, answered a question during his one visit to the United States in 1962. Knowing that he had just published a multi-volume set of *Church Dogmatics,* a person in the audience asked the author if he would summarize his theology in a single sentence. Barth thought for a moment and said, "Jesus loves me, this I know, for the Bible tells me so."

The title for the book you hold in your hands – *Three Simple Truths* – emerged after I became acquainted with two volumes by Rueben Job: *Three Simple Rules* and *Three Simple Questions*. I maintained the words "three" and "simple" and coupled them with the word "truths" because the three statements are more than affirmations. Millions of people in churches around the world believe these statements to be true. So do I.

Those who are adherents of other religious traditions may also find one, two, or all three of the statements to be an expression of their faith. This is particularly valid for those in the Jewish community since they embrace a substantial portion of the Christian Bible. Many passages I quote in this book are from their scriptures, especially the Psalms.

Three Simple Truths is an outgrowth of my relationship with God, and my reflections on that relationship. However, as essential as personal experience is, it is not sufficient. Only when people interact with others, both within and beyond their community of faith, can meaningful theological assertions surface for discussion and revision. Only then can beliefs emerge that are highly likely to be true, and thereby called "truths."

Some of the most important conversation partners in my life—in addition to my wife, Naomi, other members of my family, and my close friends—are a number of colleagues who have influenced my thinking in substantial ways. Most significant during my academic training were Edward Blair, Samuel Laeuchli, Milo Rediger, Ernest Saunders, and Robert Traina. Equally important have been professional peers such as Herbert Cassel, Michael Coyner, Neal Fisher, Robert Jewett, Lallene Rector, Wolfgang Roth, and John Wimmer. I thank them and many others for their contributions to my theological formulations. I also thank Holly Miller for her editorial assistance, Brenda Freije for her musical collaboration, and several other colleagues who have read and commented on all or a part of this volume: Madeline Arnott, Rick Arnott, Jan Blaising, Herb Cassel, Sara Cobb, Mike Coyner, Neal Fisher, Brenda Freije, Jeremiah Gibbs, Naomi Hansen, Jill Moffett Howard, Jay Kesler, Lallene Rector, and Chris Thornsberry. Finally, I am grateful to the team at Inkwater Press – particularly Sean Jones, Masha Shubin, and John Williams – who have assisted me in so many thoughtful ways in the production of this volume.

INTRODUCTION:
DISCERNING THESE TRUTHS

Stuff happens every day! The news media show it in pictures, speak about it in words – every hour of every day. Often the "stuff" takes place in other people's lives, but sometimes it occurs in our own lives. It can come about gradually – like a gathering storm some distance away – or it can strike suddenly – like a bolt of lightning.

Stuff happens to all of us in one way or another. And when it does, what do we think? What do we say? How does it make us feel? Does it prompt celebration? Or does it cause devastation? Or something in-between?

(PAUSE TO REFLECT)

When the stuff brings us joy, or a mixture of joy and sadness, we have little difficulty dealing with it. But when it brings sadness – especially pain and anguish, we suffer intellectually, physically, emotionally, and spiritually. We don't know what to think. We don't know how to act. We don't know what to feel. And most significantly for many of us, we don't know where God is in the midst of the trauma.

This book is an attempt to comprehend more fully who God is, how God acts, and what God offers, especially in tough times. It expresses my viewpoint on the basis of scripture (quoted frequently), tradition (identified numerous times), reason (utilized throughout), and experience (named and shared in explicit ways).

The three words of the title permeate the organization of the book. Each chapter sets forth one of the truths, discusses it word by word, and then concludes with a group of exercises that includes a series of questions, a cluster of practices, a prayer, and a list of suggestions pertaining to the musical refrain that appears at the end.

The lyrics in each musical selection are set forth in an ABBA pattern which state the truth, and then restate it in reverse form. The music comes from folk tunes that people can easily sing or hum.

A postscript follows the three main sections. In it I attempt to share, as honestly as I can, how I have experienced these truths – as a child, a college student, and an adult. In doing so, I hope that you – the readers – will examine your own lives, discern how you have experienced these truths, and then share your witness with others.

I've based the illustrations at the end of each chapter on actual events, though in chapters one and three I have changed names and a few insignificant details to protect the identity of those whose experiences I have described. The illustration in chapter two is already public knowledge.

My interest is that this book will appeal to a wide audience. Children, youth, and adults of all ages can learn and recite the truths and sing the musical selections that express them. Entire families can utilize them in informal as well as more formal gatherings. Church school classes for children, youth, and adults can incorporate them in their respective curricula. Churches can include them in a variety of worship settings.

When children learn verses from the Bible, prayers from an ecclesial tradition, or truths as set forth in this book, such memorizations are likely to stay with them into youth and adulthood. This has been true in my life – time and time again. For example, when my parents encouraged me to memorize the 23rd Psalm as a child, I didn't realize how those words would become a powerful source of strength when my daughter was killed. A few days after her funeral in Indianapolis, I shared the opening words of that Psalm with the seminary community in Evanston, Illinois, just prior to a chapel service. With tears in my eyes I said: "The Lord is **still** my shepherd." Those were the only words I could get out before tears choked my throat and I had to sit down. What I had learned as a child became my anchor in the midst of a raging storm!

Children of almost any age can learn these truths. They can recite them either in a sentence or as a responsive dialogue – with a brother, sister, mother, father, or any other person in a conversation. They can sing them or hum them – by themselves or in a group. They can do this at home, church, or another setting. And children too young to participate can listen to a caregiver sing or hum the melodies.

Youth and adults can do the same. They can even invite others, younger and older, to participate. In addition, they can discuss what the truths mean, without reciting them or singing them at all. These truths can permeate life – at any time and at specific points in time – in families, churches, and a variety of gatherings in the community – even in a hospital room or a funeral visitation alcove.

Not only will the truths in this book relate to persons of varying ages and circumstances, they will also resonate with people who are Evangelicals, Moderates, and Progressives within Protestantism, as well as those who are Roman Catholic or Orthodox. Of course interpretations will vary, but the truths will connect with each of these constituencies. Other faiths may also participate in the conversation in order to foster communication and seek points of commonality.

In an attempt to be sensitive to the perspective of those of other faiths who may read this book, I have used abbreviations that are becoming customary, namely, BCE (Before the Common Era) and CE (the Common Era), rather than BC (Before Christ) and AD (Anno Domini) to distinguish dates. It is difficult, sometimes impossible, for persons to say AD because the words contained in that affirmation – "in the year of the Lord" – is a statement of faith. Although I would prefer to use the terms "First" and "Second" for the two "Testaments" of the Bible – particularly since many of the references in this book come from the First Testament – I have chosen to employ the terms "Old" and "New" because they are familiar designations for many who will read this book.

When we speak of truth, it is imperative that we establish its source. Many possibilities exist. However, in a book as brief as this, we will consider one understanding as primary and sufficient, namely, that *God is the source of all truth!* This means we don't have to be afraid of pursuing truth, since all truth will lead us to God – if indeed it is truth. Whether we discover truth in a laboratory through a microscope, or in an observatory through a telescope, it will not lead us away from God. Regardless of what the truth is, who discovers it, where it comes from, when it is found, and how it is uncovered, it will lead us to, and not from, God. What a solid foundation! What a source of comfort and strength!

In this book we are dealing with "three simple truths." There could be many more, but a larger number would mean a longer discussion. Furthermore, such an approach would likely require an increasing level of complexity – one that would include additional theoretical abstraction. That is not what I intend in this volume. Neither is a number fewer than three, for that would narrow the scope of the discussion to such an extent that meaning would diminish.

The use of the word "simple" suggests that most persons – even at a young age – will be able to grasp the meaning of the three sentences that comprise the titles of the chapters. They are not complicated, elaborate, pretentious statements. Rather, they are ordinary, common, and straightforward.

At the same time, these truths are deeply significant. They are profound when we state them, but even more profound when we experience them. For there is a great deal of power in lived truth, far more than in abstract truth. And that's why the subtitle of the book reads: "EXPERIENCING THEM IN OUR LIVES."

The word "truths" is more difficult to define than "three" or "simple," especially in such a limited discussion. Space doesn't allow us to analyze theories of truth, as important as they may be. Neither is space available to examine claims regarding "absolute truth," or "propositional truth," or "objective/subjective truth." Such categories of abstraction are not central to our discussion. Our focus is on experiencing these truths in our lives.

The place of "community" in determining truth is – in my judgment – of paramount importance. It begins with the development of our individual identities in the context of a group we call "family" – whatever the composition might be: small or large, traditional or non-traditional, single or multi-generational. In any case, it's a community. It's the context in which our initial beliefs and values emerge.

The stories of our lives are embedded in the stories of the communities from which we derive our identities; and in this discussion, the "faith communities" of which we are a part, beginning with the people of Israel who are known to us – historically – through the Old Testament. Members of the community told stories of their relationship with God, with each other, and with those outside their group. They acted out their stories in rituals. And to preserve their way of life, they recorded their experiences and beliefs in a series of writings (in Hebrew) that were collected, handed down to subsequent generations, and eventually became known as the "Law" (by 400 BCE), the "Prophets" (by 200 BCE), and the "Writings" (by 90 CE). The truths recorded in these writings became authoritative for what the community was to believe and how the community was to live.

With the birth of Jesus (ca. 6 BCE) and the ministry he carried out with 12 disciples (ca. 24-27 CE), a new faith community formed. Those who were a part of this initial following of Jesus were Jewish – as was Jesus – and were connected to that faith community. They experienced "truths" by how Jesus lived, taught, healed, died, and was raised from the dead.

Followers of Jesus continued to develop their faith community after the death and resurrection of Jesus, and wrote down (in Greek) what they were experiencing. The Apostle Paul wrote a series of letters (late 40s and 50s). Others wrote Gospels: Mark (late 60s), Matthew and Luke (80s), and John (90s). Luke also wrote a second volume, the Acts of the Apostles (80s). John wrote an Apocalypse (90s). Still others wrote additional Epistles (60s-120s).

These writings circulated among a number of small faith communities located in the Western portion of the Roman Empire (areas we know today as Israel, Turkey, Greece, and Italy). As they were read and heard over and over again, as they were identified with one of the apostles, and as lives were transformed, they became recognized as authoritative. First there were four Gospels, Acts, and some of Paul's Letters (by the end of the second century). Then a few additional writings were added (by the early fourth century). Finally, in 367 CE, a list of all 27 books emerged as the canonical writings for the faith community known as the Church – the collection that came to be known as the New Testament.

The early centuries of the Church, and those that followed, continued to determine what were authoritative truths. The most important influences were the canonical writings of two testaments, the creedal formulations of ecumenical councils, the beliefs and practices of the Eastern and Western churches (following the schism of 1054), the reform movements that took place – particularly the Protestant Reformation that became notable in 1517 – and the ongoing process of denominational formations.

Throughout these twenty centuries during which the Church was in the process of defining and living out its faith, debate after debate took place regarding what truths Christians ought to believe and practice. Certain truths became more prominent than others, and it is out of these truths that three emerged for examination in this book, each being analyzed by means of scripture, tradition, reason, and experience.

These three truths are not individualistic; neither are they private. Their authority grows out of the faith community in which they are rooted – the Church of past generations, and the Church of the present. They are communal and can therefore be called "communal truths."

Experiencing these truths is not simply giving mental assent to them; it is incarnating them in our lives. They are not built on intellectual certainty; they grow out of a relationship with God – a trust relationship that can provide psychological certainty, though not absolute certainty. This does not make the process "anti-intellectual." No, the intellect engages as fully as possible, but in the final analysis, it comes down to trust – without proof – in a God who is good all the time, and who works for good in everything. These truths are relational and can therefore be called "relational truths."

A psalmist asks God to help him in this process: "Make known to me your ways, Lord; teach me your paths; lead me in your *truth*" (25:4-5). So does the writer of the hymn, "Open My Eyes, that I May See" (United Methodist Hymnal, 454), when she prays: "Open my eyes, that I may see glimpses of *truth* thou hast for me" (verse 1) – "Open my ears, that I may hear voices of *truth* thou sendest clear" (verse 2) – "Open my mouth, and let me bear gladly the warm *truth* everywhere" (verse 3). I join with them and invite you to do the same.

CHAPTER 1

God Is Good, All the Time

All the Time, God Is Good

CHARACTER OF GOD

"God is good;
his steadfast love endures forever,
and his faithfulness to all generations."

Psalm 100:5

The "first simple truth" is well known in many circles across the theological spectrum: Evangelicals, Moderates, and Progressives recite it from memory. Most often a leader begins by saying, "God is good." The congregation responds, "all the time." The leader repeats the words, "all the time," and the congregation responds, " God is good."

This truth has only six words: a subject (God), a verb (is), a predicate adjective (good), and a categorical phrase (all the time). Yet they convey a great deal of meaning. They reveal the character of God, not simply an attribute of God.

The interpretation we give these words may vary in its application to life, but we understand them in a rather uniform manner, particularly the first three words. The last three words lead to a variety of understandings as persons attempt to relate them to different sets of circumstances.

GOD

What do you think about when you hear the word "God?" Is it a religious thought – one that is related to a community of faith? Is it an everyday idiom – one that might show up in social media as "OMG?" Or is it a vulgar expression that someone blurts out when very angry?

(PAUSE TO REFLECT)

Most of us in the English-speaking world use the word "God" to refer to the divine. Some in the Jewish tradition employ the Hebrew word *Adonai* in biblical and liturgical readings, even when the biblical text says *Yahweh,* since that name is considered too holy and sacred to say aloud.

Others in the Christian tradition say the Greek word *Theos,* particularly in the Orthodox Church, whether the ethnicity is Greek, Armenian, Syrian, or some other. The Latin word *Deus* is also spoken, especially in highly liturgical services in the Roman Catholic Church.

Still others, who call upon God in their own traditions and in their own native languages, use words such as *Dios* (Spanish), *Dieu* (French), *Gott* (German), *Gud* (Norwegian), *Allah* (Arabic), *Kami* (Japanese), or *Tanri* (Turkish).

In addition to various names for God, we interpret God in differing ways. One of these is an "impersonal" understanding. For example, if we use the category of "being," we can speak of God in terms of "being as being," as the ancient Greek philosopher, Aristotle, did (fourth century BCE), or the "ground of being," as the recent German theologian, Paul Tillich, did (twentieth century CE).

Another understanding in the Christian tradition – a far more common one – is a "personal" understanding. Continuing to use the category of "being," we can affirm that God is a personal being. However, in doing so, we do not have to define God. We can, instead, describe God. And these two approaches differ greatly!

Defining God is simply not possible. God is infinite. That is, God is without limits and without boundaries. On the other hand, human beings are finite. They have limits and boundaries. And, as finite creatures, we find it impossible to define an infinite creator.

What is incredibly exciting, and profoundly meaningful, is that we can experience God as a personal being, even though God is far more than that. If we try to say this in words that define God in a personal category, we might say that God is supra-personal; that is, God is understood as transcending or reaching beyond a personal being. However, that does not result in a great deal of excitement, or a deep level of meaning.

In the Christian tradition we believe we can *experience* God as a personal being. This means we can enter into a relationship with God – the One whom we can experience as a personal being.

Yes, God by definition is far more than a personal being. God is not the smile at the side of the crib that a child growing up projects on a cosmic screen in his or her adult years. No, God is not an anthropomorphic projection of an inner need or urge. God is simply one who relates to us in such a way that we can *experience* God as a personal being, even when we understand that God, by definition, is far more than a personal being.

What makes this more profound, and more powerful, is that God chose to enter history and make himself known through a personal being – a human being – named Jesus. However, this doesn't mean Jesus is like God. It means God is like Jesus!

The primary reason Jesus came to earth was to show human beings what God is like. In doing so, he was born as a human being, lived until his early 30s, taught many significant "truths," brought salvation/healing/wholeness to people, died for us and for others, and was raised from the dead.

Furthermore, since Jesus not only "was" here on earth, but also – because of his resurrection – "is" here on earth, we can have a relationship with him. And, because we can have a relationship with him, we can also have a relationship with God, since Jesus came to show us what God is like. This is what Jesus is explaining to Philip when he says: "Whoever has seen me has seen the Father" (John 14:9-10).

As we try to understand who God is in the Christian tradition, we can try to comprehend how there can be one God, yet three persons – what is often called the "triune Godhead" or the "trinity." Such a perspective is a matter we can't clearly explain to ourselves and/or to others, but solid affirmations grow out of the Bible and the tradition of the Christian Church that we can identify.

To state it in a very general manner, we can say that the overall development of an understanding of God in the Western world began with polytheism (many gods), then moved to henotheism (one God above the other gods), and finally to monotheism (one God, and only one). This belief in one God was – and is – central to Jewish theology.

References in the Old Testament (also known as the Hebrew Bible, or the Tanach) repeatedly state that there is only one God. The most familiar verse is called the *Shema*: "Hear, O Israel, the Lord is one God, the Lord alone" (Deuteronomy 6:14). The 10 Commandments (Exodus 20:2-17 and Deuteronomy 5:6-21) as well as numerous other passages confirm this.

Such an understanding of monotheism was carried into the Christian faith, namely, that there is one God, and only one. Yet the inclusion of Jesus into this interpretation created considerable difficulty for the emerging Christian Church. How could people uphold monotheism and, at the same time, recognize the risen Christ as God?

What led the Church to affirm a triune Godhead was their conviction that the God they knew through the Old Testament was none other than the God they encountered in Jesus Christ, as well as the God whom they experienced in the Holy Spirit – the presence that continued with them following the resurrection. Their encounter with Jesus Christ was not just exemplary humanity. The experience of the Holy Spirit following the resurrection was not just emotional afterglow. It was the one and the same God who approached them in all three forms. The triune Godhead was an expression of confidence in the one God encountering them in three different ways.

For the first five centuries CE, leaders in the Christian Church debated these matters, proposed a variety of explanations, and decided each of these had one or more heretical flaws in them. They finally decided to affirm that the earthly Jesus and the risen Christ were one and the same, and, without fully explaining it, declared that Jesus is both human and divine.

A different understanding of God and Jesus also emerged in the early centuries, a perspective that continues to this day. It is most commonly known as Unitarianism. Those who believe in this view affirm that God is one, and that Jesus was not divine. They say that claiming Jesus as divine would be a threat to the monotheism they affirm. They understand Jesus as a human being filled with God's spirit more fully than anyone else. His difference from other human beings is one of degree, not kind. He taught many significant "truths," brought healing and wholeness to people, died, but was not raised from the dead.

Trinitarianism, on the other hand, affirms that there is one God, but goes on to explain that there is a "triune Godhead." This means three comprise the "Godhead," namely, the Father (sometimes called Creator), Son (sometimes called Redeemer), and Holy Spirit (sometimes called Sustainer). None of these three is God in his own right. They are God when they are combined—when they are joined together.

In this interpretation, Jesus is one who is both divine and human – a belief firmly claimed, but not readily explained. Although finite creatures have attempted in all sorts of ways to delineate how this is possible, God – who is infinite – continues to be beyond satisfactory human comprehension.

Those of us who are Trinitarian express this belief in worship on a regular basis. We sing the Doxology and say in the last line, "Praise Father, Son, and Holy Ghost." We also sing the Gloria and declare, "Glory be to the Father, and to the Son, and to the Holy Ghost." And we make the same declarations in other hymns we sing as we affirm the divinity of Jesus Christ.

One of these hymns is often sung during the Christmas season: "Come and worship, come and worship, worship Christ, the newborn King" (UMH, 220). These words and those in numerous other hymns are based on the understanding that Jesus Christ is divine as well as human. For example, one hymn states this very clearly: "We believe in one true God, Father, Son, and Holy Ghost" (UMH, 85). In another hymn, one verse says, "Holy Father, Holy Son, Holy Spirit: three we name thee, though in essence only one; undivided God we claim thee, and adoring bend the knee while we own the mystery" (UMH, 79). In still another, the words identify Jesus as divine in a very explicit manner: "Majesty, worship his majesty; unto Jesus be all glory, honor, and praise" (UMH, 176).

In addition, numerous Easter hymns celebrate Jesus having been raised from the dead, and continuing to live in the present. Examples are: "He is risen from the dead and he is Lord" (UMH, 177); "He lives" (UMH, 310); and "Because he lives I can face tomorrow" (UMH, 364).

The words in these hymns and many others are based on the understanding that Jesus Christ is both human and divine. This makes it difficult for persons who don't believe he is divine to sing such hymns with the same meaning as those who do. These hymns are composed for singers to worship the triune Godhead and, in doing so, to worship the risen Lord. Those who don't believe Jesus Christ is divine don't worship him; for it would be idolatrous to do so.

Trinitarians believe Jesus Christ is one person whom we experience in two ways. We experience the earthly Jesus (using the name he was called) when we read about him in the Bible, particularly in Matthew, Mark, Luke, and John. However, when we read about Jesus after his resurrection, we experience him as the risen Christ (the Annointed One – the Messiah).

The Christian Church has a number of creedal formulations. The earliest one is called the Nicene Creed – initially formulated in 325 CE at the Council of Nicaea, though the version that is commonly used is the one that was modified in 381 CE at the Council of Constantinople (UMH, 880). Another formulation, the Apostles Creed, comes from the eighth century CE in the form we now have it, though its roots date back to earlier centuries (UMH, 881 and 882).

These creeds are clearly Trinitarian, affirming belief in the triune Godhead by means of individual sections dealing with Father, Son, and Holy Spirit. More modern creeds have a greater variety of theological expression, though they still make reference to God the Father, Jesus Christ, and the Holy Spirit (UMH, 884 and 885).

Earlier than any of these formulations are the affirmations of faith in the New Testament, particularly Romans 8:35, 37-39 (UMH, 887); 1 Corinthians 15:1-6 and Colossians 1:15-20 (UMH, 888); and 1 Timothy 1:15; 2:5-6; 3:16 (UMH, 889). These and other passages contain indicators of a triune Godhead, though the more widely accepted theological formulations had not yet been developed.

IS

When you see a section of a chapter with a two-letter verb as a title, does it make you wonder if it's important enough to warrant such prominence? Is it merely a connection between a subject and a predicate adjective? Or is the significance greater than that?

(PAUSE TO REFLECT)

Part of the significance of this verb is its present tense—commonly understood as continuous action. It differs from those tenses that refer to a particular action at a certain point in time.

When utilized in the sentence of this chapter, it is a verb that describes the character of God as an ongoing quality, one that has been in the past, continues in the present, and is anticipated in the future. However, making clear what the character of God is in the present does not make a claim about what God's character will necessarily be in the future. It is simply a declarative word about the present. Whether God's character might change in the future is dependent on whether God can change his character. If God is all-powerful, and thereby has the freedom to make decisions in a limitless matter, can God change who God is? Is there any guarantee that God must – by some outside necessity – remain constant in character? Or, can God act out of character? Yes, these are only theoretical questions. However, they may very well be worth considering. For, if God could change in character, but doesn't, we have all the more reason to praise God!

The good news is that God has remained constant in character in the past and has continued to remain constant in character up to the present moment. Therefore, God is highly likely to be constant in character into the future. And, although we cannot prove that this will be, we can trust God that it will be. And, in doing so, we can praise God for not changing in character!

Numerous passages in the Bible declare who God "is." An example is Psalm 100:5 where the writer says, "*God is good*; his steadfast love endures forever, and his faithfulness to all generations." In the four verses preceding this affirmation, the reader is invited to "make a joyful noise," to "worship with gladness," to "enter gates with thanksgiving and courts with praise," and to "give thanks." And then the word "for" follows at the beginning of verse 5, indicating the reason why the reader ought to do this, namely, "for God is . . ." which is significant enough in and of itself, but much more powerful when the word "good" is added.

GOOD

When you ask a person, "How are you?" and the answer is "I'm good," you probably assume that person means "I'm well." When you ask a dinner guest in your home, "Would you like some more?" and the answer is "I'm good," you probably know that person is saying, "No."

It's interesting how those words – "I'm good" – have become a common expression that is generally unrelated to the issue of moral character. But when we think about God's character, and we assert that God is good, are we thinking of a moral quality?

(PAUSE TO REFLECT)

Many theologians across the centuries have debated what the word "good" means, particularly as it relates to God. They have developed and debated a variety of interpretations that often involve considerable philosophical analysis. Rather than engage in those conversations, we're going to reflect on the word "good" from the perspective of the Psalmist who declares that "*God is good*; his steadfast love endures forever." We're not going to define what we mean by "good" and then determine whether or not God's character fits within it.

To put this into historical context, let's remember the opening declaration God gave to Moses as he was about to renew his covenant with the people of Israel: "The Lord, a God merciful and gracious, slow to anger, and abounding in steadfast love and faithfulness" (Exodus 34:6). These covenantal words were spoken centuries before the Psalms were written and provided a foundation – both historically and literarily – for what they were going to say.

The words "steadfast love" come from one Hebrew word, *hesed* (sometimes spelled *chesed* to signify the guttural pronunciation of the first letter), often translated in the Greek Septuagint as *eleos*. It is a key term for several reasons, one of which is its frequent use in the Hebrew Old Testament: 247 times. And, because of its frequent usage, it carried with it a great deal of meaning. Or, perhaps just the reverse, namely, because of its depth of meaning, it became used over and over and over again. Or, perhaps both.

In the Five Books of Psalms – a total of 150 Psalms – the word *hesed* shows up 127 times. And what is remarkable within that number is that it is used 26 times in an antiphonal Psalm, once in each verse (Psalm 136). The other 101 times are scattered throughout the other Psalms. While there are various nuances of meaning in the respective contexts in which this word is used, the basic understanding is essentially the same.

Translators have offered other words – in addition to "steadfast love" – for the word *hesed*. Some of these are mercy or merciful, loving-kindness, compassion, and a variety of modifiers to the word "love" such as faithful, loyal, extravagant.

Although not strictly translations, others have modified the word "love" with words such as unconditional, unqualified, unrestricted, unreserved, and unconstrained – words that are more Greco-Roman than Hebraic in their root meaning. While these convey some of the same meaning as "steadfast," they do not carry the same level of energy and strength. Neither does the word "love" when it is used without any modifier. The translation of *hesed* that is used consistently by the editors of the New Revised Standard Version (as well as the Revised Standard Version) is "steadfast love." It is found in many books of the Bible in addition to the Psalms: Genesis, Exodus, Numbers, Deuteronomy, 2 Samuel, 1 Kings, 1 Chronicles, 2 Chronicles, Ezra, Nehemiah, Job, Isaiah, Jeremiah, Lamentations, Daniel, Hosea, Joel, and Jonah.

Steadfast love is at the core of God's character. It is the way we are defining the word "good" in this volume. When we say, "God is good," we are not only saying "God is love" as some translations do. We are saying, "God is steadfast love" – a more dynamic and powerful expression of love.

The Psalms offer various descriptions of steadfast love. One of these deepens its meaning: "The Lord is gracious and merciful, slow to anger and abounding in *steadfast love*. The Lord is *good* to all, and his compassion is over all that he has made" (145:8). Another broadens its scope: "Your *steadfast love* is higher than the heavens, and your faithfulness reaches to the clouds" (108:4). Still another sets forth its inclusive character: "All the paths of the Lord are *steadfast love* and faithfulness" (25:10).

There are also a variety of ways the significance of steadfast love is expressed. A first one articulates its value: "How precious is your *steadfast love*, O God! All people may take refuge in the shadow of your wings" (36:7). A second connects it to faithfulness: "*Steadfast love* and faithfulness will meet; righteousness and peace will kiss each other. Faithfulness will spring up from the ground, and righteousness will look down from the sky. The Lord will give what is *good*" (85:10). A third delineates its abundance: "You, O Lord, are a God merciful and gracious, slow to anger and abounding in *steadfast love* and faithfulness" (86:15).

In addition, several verses describe the effect steadfast love has on people. One of these is the vision it provides: "Your *steadfast love* is before my eyes, and I will walk in faithfulness to you" (26:3). One more is the comfort it gives: "Let your *steadfast love* become my comfort according to your promise to your servant" (119:76). Still one more is the sustaining presence it offers: "Because your *steadfast love* is better than life, my lips will praise you. So I will bless you as long as I live; I will lift up my hands and call on your name" (63:3).

Beyond these verses, others include steadfast love as part of a prayer. One is in a confession: "Have mercy on me, O God, according to your *steadfast love*; according to your abundant mercy blot out my transgressions. Wash me thoroughly from my iniquity, and cleanse me from my sin" (51:1-2). Another is in a supplication: "You, O Lord, are *good* and forgiving, abounding in *steadfast love* to all who call on you. Give ear, O Lord, to my prayer; listen to my cry of supplication. In the day of trouble I call on you, for you will answer me" (86:5).

This last reference contains the explicit affirmation that is directed to God: "You, O Lord, are *good* and forgiving, abounding in *steadfast love*." In other words, the psalmist connects "good" and "steadfast love," thereby making it clear that when we say, "God is good," we also are affirming, "God is steadfast love."

Consistent with such an interpretation, psalmists also provide responses to steadfast love. For example, one Psalm offers praise: "Blessed be the Lord, for he has wondrously shown his *steadfast love* to me" (31:21). Three separate Psalms encourage thanksgiving: "O give thanks to the Lord, for he is *good*; for his *steadfast love* endures forever" (106:1; 107:1; 118:1). And another Psalm gives an exhortation that looks to the future: "Let your *steadfast love*, O Lord, be upon us, even as we hope in you" (33:2).

ALL THE TIME

When a person asks another, "Do you drive within the speed limit that's posted?" The response may be "all the time." But both persons know this is a tongue-in-cheek answer, one that leads to smiles and winks.

When a person unexpectedly meets a friend at the mall and inquires, "Do you come here often?" the answer may be "all the time." And such a response is more believable, though it may be an overstatement.

When a person is wearing a T-shirt with the name of a particular football team, someone might point to the name and ask, "Do you root for this team?" The answer is likely to be "all the time." And such a response may very well be true.

The phrase "all the time" can have various meanings that range from what is not really true, to what is sometimes true, to what is likely true. However, it also can affirm something that is always true – without any exception whatsoever! Is this what "all the time" means when it refers to the character of God? In short, is God *always* good – regardless of what the situation might be?

(PAUSE TO REFLECT)

When we are going through change, we may not even think about whether or not God is changing. In other words, when our circumstances absorb our time, our energy, and our outlook, we may become so focused on ourselves that we live "as if" there was no God at all. And, at those times, the thought of whether or not God is changing, or remaining the same, doesn't cross our minds.

When life is going well, we may remember – at least some of the time – that God is good. But when life is not going well, we may or may not remember that God is still good. For example, when we're experiencing an illness – particularly a serious one – or when we've lost a job, or when a relationship has broken up, or when a family member or close friend has died, we may forget that God is good.

However, our forgetting that God is good, or even denying that God is good, doesn't change the character of God. God remains good – all the time!

The significance of this for us is not only that God remains good, but also that God is with us – all the time – regardless of what we may be going through. We can be confident of this. We can be assured that God's steadfast love is *always* with us. For Jesus, the one who came to show us what God is like, declared this to his disciples when he spoke to them after he was raised from the dead: "Remember, I am with you *always*, to the end of the age" (Matthew 28:20).

This means God will continually express his character – his steadfast love – toward us throughout our lives and beyond, even to the end of the entire historical process. God has promised to do this, both when we want God to be with us, and when we don't (i.e., when we don't want God to know what we're thinking, or what we're doing).

Nevertheless, the God of steadfast love is *always* – not sometimes – with us. And nothing can separate us from that love. The apostle Paul puts it this way: "I am convinced that neither death, nor life, nor angels, nor rulers, nor things present, nor things to come, nor powers, nor height, nor depth, nor anything else in all creation, will be able to separate us from the love of God in Christ Jesus our Lord" (Romans 8:38-39).

You may wonder how such an understanding of this simple truth – **God is good all the time** – can make a difference in a person's life. Here's an illustration from a real-life situation:

Jane, age 24, was living in a city in Illinois where she had spent her teenage years. She had returned to this location to accept a very desirable job, after attending college in California.

However, the move caused Jane to experience a great deal of inner turmoil. The return to familiar surroundings brought back vivid memories of her childhood and early adolescent years when her father and her older brother had taken advantage of her—over and over again—and sexually molested her. She thought she had worked through this trauma in the time she had been away. Nevertheless, returning to a place where she occasionally saw one or both of the men, stirred her feelings of anger and resentment.

By this time in her life, Jane had given up her faith in God as well as men. And she was increasingly realizing she had to get away from the place her family lived.

Jane shared the idea of moving back to California with a woman who had been one of her close friends in college and received a very welcoming response. Within a few months Jane had found a job, a place to live, and was happily developing friendships with a large cohort of thoughtful and caring women. Over several months she came to trust them and eventually revealed what she had experienced in her youth. Reliving those experiences of anguish and torment was difficult, but they also became the means to a slow, but steady healing.

One of the women who also had been deeply hurt by a man some years before, told Jane that her relationship with God had been impacted so severely that it was eventually destroyed. But she also shared that, over a period of years, she had come to the realization that it was a man, not God, who was responsible for those wretched ways; and that God was continuing to love her with a pure and steadfast love, even when she was turning her back on God.

During a period that lasted almost eight years, Jane learned from her friend, slowly found healing from her horrendous upbringing, and experienced a renewed relationship with God. She finally was able to say, "Yes, God loved me steadfastly all these years. I wish I had realized it sooner."

UNDERSTANDING IT

QUESTIONS

Responding to the following questions is one means of comprehending this truth more fully.

First, review what you've read:

- What is the writer's understanding of the words – "God" – "is" – "good" – "all the time" – in this chapter?
- To what extent do you agree or disagree with this understanding?

Second, relate what you've read to your own life:

- How would you put your understanding into your own words?
- What feelings would you associate with your understanding?
- In what ways have you already experienced this truth?
- How do you think you will experience this truth in the months and years to come?

Third, connect your understanding, your feelings, your experience, and your expectations regarding this truth with others – individually or in a group.

Formulating your own questions is another means – perhaps a more effective one.

Reflecting on the questions you've formulated and discussing them with others is still another possibility.

PRACTICES

There are various ways to express truth #1 verbally, whether in church, at home, or some other setting in the community:

Memorize it as a single sentence, or two separate phrases.

Recite the sentence by itself, or each phrase as a call and response. (Consider saying it responsively at a dinner during Advent, perhaps your Christmas dinner – if you have one – or at another time that may be more suitable.)

Write out for yourself what the truth means to you, including examples of how you understand it (in your heart and in your head), as well as how it has become a part of your life.

Share with someone else what you think it means, how it makes you feel, and ways it has become a part of your life. (Consider sharing with the same group.)

Have someone else – either an individual or a group – **share** with you and others what they think it means, how it makes them feel, and how they have experienced it. (Consider inviting others from the same group to share.)

Utilize it in your everyday activities, whether you meditate on it, say it aloud to a family member or friend, or mention it in a group setting.

PRAYERS

Making use of the following words is one manner of praying:

Gracious God, we thank you that

you are good,

your steadfast love is good, and

your steadfast love endures . . . forever.

Loving God, we thank you that

you are good all the time,

your steadfast love is good all the time, and

your steadfast love endures . . . forever.

Help us, O God, to understand this

as we think about it,

as we talk about it with you and with others, and

as we express it in our lives . . . day by day by day.

Through Jesus Christ we pray. Amen.

Composing a prayer in your own words is another method – perhaps even a more meaningful one.

M U S I C *– as found on the next page*
There are various ways to express truth #1 musically – in unison or in harmony – whether it is in church, at home, or in some other setting in the community:

Sing it by yourself or in a group.
(Consider inviting the same group to join in singing.)

Hum it by yourself or in a group.

Teach others to sing and/or hum it.

Record it, or have it recorded by someone else, and then play it for others to hear.

God Is Good, All the Time

God is good, God is good, all the time. All the time, all the time, God is good.

Words: Anon
Music: Folk Melody, arr. Adolf Hansen
© 2013 Adolf Hansen

CHAPTER 2

GOD WORKS FOR GOOD, IN EVERYTHING

IN EVERYTHING, GOD WORKS FOR GOOD

ACTIVITY OF GOD

"God works for good in everything,
with those who love God,
who are called according to his purpose."

Romans 8:28

The "second simple truth," as expressed in this book, is not well known in circles across the theological spectrum. However, the verse from which it originates is quite familiar to Evangelicals, Moderates, and Progressives, though many of them express it in other ways. They rarely recite it in a responsive manner with the leader saying, "God works for good," and the congregation responding, "in everything," followed by the leader repeating the words, "in everything," and the congregation responding, "God works for good."

Like the "first truth," this one has six words: a subject (God), a verb (works), an object (for good), and a categorical phrase (in everything). Although the truth is short in length, the words express a profound level of meaning. They portray the overall way God works, not simply one of the ways.

The manner in which these words relate to life situations may vary, but the core understanding is commonly accepted, particularly the first four words. The last two words open possibilities for persons to apply them to their own circumstances.

GOD

In chapter one you were asked what you thought about when you heard the word "God." And then you were given three items to consider: names that are often used for God, a description of God as a personal being, and an understanding of God as a triune Godhead.

In this chapter we continue our thinking about God as we consider some of the ways God expresses his character of steadfast love. And there are many! Does any particular one come to mind?

(PAUSE TO REFLECT)

The first one we'll explore is the way God exercises power. We won't have to spend much time making a case for the affirmation that God is powerful. Evidence of this permeates the history of Christian tradition. Verses from the Bible declare it in no uncertain terms. For example, "Great is our Lord, and abundant in power; his understanding is beyond measure" (Psalm 147:5). Another verse – particularly interesting in this discussion – connects power to steadfast love: "Hope in the Lord! For with the Lord there is steadfast love, and with him is great power to redeem" (Psalm 130:7). And beyond the Bible are statements that refer to God's power in our prayers ("Thine is the power" in the Lord's Prayer), in our creedal formulations ("God the Father, Almighty"), and in our hymns ("Praise to the Lord, the Almighty").

However, when we think about how God exercises power in relation to the world, the picture is less clear. The basis on which God does this is not always self-evident. God sometimes chooses to act in a way that does not bring about the highest expression of what God wants.

God gives human beings freedom to choose and, in doing so, *God limits himself.* For God does not, and will not, take away the freedom God has given. This means many things take place in life that are not the highest expression of what God wants. For example, we are free to hurt one another. God does not stop us. God is not able to stop us unless he takes away the freedom that makes us human.

God wants us to have freedom of choice. And God wants us to make desirable choices – the highest expression of what God wants. Nevertheless, God is willing to give up his highest expression in exchange for a lesser one, namely, the ability of human beings to have freedom of choice.

Furthermore, choice is a necessity if we are going to love God – not because we have to, but because we choose to. In other words, without such freedom, human beings would not be able to love God, or other human beings.

At the same time, we can affirm that God can intervene. God has the power to do so. God is sovereign and is thereby not limited by any outside source. However, God chooses not to intervene in any way that will negate our freedom. God chooses to limit himself in direct proportion to the freedom God has given us. In other words, God allows – permits – many things to take place that do not end up with the result God would like to see (i.e., the highest expression of what God wants).

This manner of functioning is not very different from parents who give their children freedom to learn on their own; freedom to make mistakes as well as freedom to do the right thing; freedom to hurt themselves when learning to climb a tree, or ride a bicycle; freedom to choose friends with values different from, or similar to, their own; freedom to act irresponsibly or responsibly with their health, their possessions, their opportunities, etc.

Parents limit themselves when they give such freedom to their children. And, in like manner, God limits himself when God gives freedom to us. Parents could withdraw the freedom their children have, but, in doing so, they would not be able to provide a context in which the children could grow into mature adults.

So it is with God. The choice to give freedom to us is a choice God could, theoretically, withdraw. That is, God could "unlimit" (i.e., overrule) what God has limited. But, if God did, we would not be able to accept, ignore, or reject God. Furthermore, we can be confident that God would never do so; for God is dependable and can be trusted to function on the basis of the freedom God has granted. God can be praised because his character remains constant!

Although God is sovereign, God doesn't express that sovereignty by determining all that takes place. God could. God has the power to do it, but God chooses not to—at least as long as human beings have the freedom to make choices.

This leads us to the second means by which God expresses his character, namely, the manner in which God controls – and doesn't control – his activity. The underlying issue is not whether God is in control, or whether God is not. It is not that simple – not that "yes or no." It is more complex than that, and it needs to be. For that is the only way to come to a satisfactory understanding of how God carries out his activity.

Most persons seem to resonate with the assertion that "God is in control." A songwriter has written a song with this title. However, we need to look at that assertion very carefully – on the one hand affirming how it is true, and on the other, how it is not.

One of the reasons we may find comfort in those words is that they assure us that life is not out of control – even when it seems to be, or at least seems to be heading in that direction. We like such an understanding because it lowers our anxiety level; increases our sense of inner peace; enables us to feel more secure; encourages us not to give up.

However, does such an affirmation fit with what we have examined, namely, that God interacts with the world in ways that include self-limitation, particularly in relation to human beings? Furthermore, does it fit with the freedom of choice we have as we participate in the life of the world?

The understanding we have been analyzing would seem to lead us to conclude that God is not in control. However, that is not quite accurate. While it is true that God does not presently exercise control in dealing with day-by-day occurrences in the world, it is also true that God will someday in the future exercise control – full and complete control – when God puts a meaningful end to history, one that is carried out through Jesus Christ.

This end to "history as we know it" is called the return of Christ, or the second coming of Christ. It will be a time when God has the final word – when righteousness is vindicated and evil is overcome. When that will be, no one knows. But it will occur, and we can look forward to it with joyful expectation. We can experience the anticipation of it now. We can be filled with a powerful hope – one that motivates and strengthens our faithfulness. For, in the final analysis, God will not be defeated!

In the meantime, God is in the process of actualizing the kingdom of God – the reign of God – in many ways. God is at work with those who are attempting to bring about justice in many areas of life: reaching out to the poor, developing economic opportunity, feeding the hungry, healing the sick, making peace, educating the masses, overcoming racism and sexism, and many other injustices embedded in systems and structures of society. However, God is limited – by God's own choosing – in what God can do. With a broken heart God allows persons to expend energy in activities that are not focused on what God is attempting to do – even activities that are contrary to what God is trying to accomplish.

Someday the reign of God will come in all its fullness. Someday God will exercise full control. But in this life, God chooses not to exercise specific day-by-day control of our lives. We can obey or disobey God; that is up to us. We can follow the teachings of Jesus, or not. We can help others or hurt others. In other words, God does not exercise control of our lives unless we allow God to do it. And even when we do, even when we earnestly ask God to take control, we fall short and feel, think, and/or act in ways not pleasing to God. We have the freedom to make choices that fit with what God is seeking to do – to a small degree, to a large degree, and even on occasion to a complete degree.

Many things happen in life that are not *caused* by God: a teenager hits a boy and injures him; a man breaks into a house and rapes a woman; a drunken driver strikes a car head on and kills its passengers. Things occur every day – all over the world – things that are not caused by God. Therefore, we can't claim that God is in control of day-by-day events in life. If we do, we end up blaming God for a lot of evil that goes on in the world.

Neither can we expect God to give us preferential treatment. If we are late to the airport and miss a flight that ends up in a crash that kills all the passengers, we need to be careful not to praise God for – somehow – keeping us off that flight so we might live. God doesn't play favorites in that way. We can praise God that we are alive – that we didn't die in that crash – but we dare not think that God loved us more than those who were killed and, as a result, kept us from taking that flight.

Neither can we presume that God gives us grace God doesn't give to others. When we see a mother and her young children standing beside the casket of her husband who was killed by a drunken driver, we may be tempted to say, "There, but for the grace of God, go I." But if we do, what are we implying? Is not the grace of God applicable to that mother as much as it is to us? Or, when we see a disheveled man begging for money, we may be thinking of that same phrase. But is not the grace of God extended to him as well as us?

Neither can we assume that everything happens for a reason. As comforting as that thought might be, many things take place without any reason. Claiming there is a reason for everything is a heavy burden to carry. It means an individual must always try to explain why something took place, and when that's not evident, he or she often experiences frustration by the inability to do so. Furthermore, it means that a person who believes God has a reason for everything, even when the reason is not apparent, makes God ultimately responsible for everything that happens, whether it's an act that's good or an act that's evil.

One way to describe many things that take place in life that are not understandable is simply to say, *"Stuff happens."* A child darts out from behind a parked car, is hit by an oncoming car, and is confined to a wheel chair for life. A teenager develops a malignant brain tumor that precipitously shortens his life. A woman is struck by shrapnel from a bomb and is disfigured to such an extent that she is barely recognizable. A foul ball hits a man in the head and causes him to lose his capacity to see and to hear. An adult is diagnosed with a terminal illness. Two people are struck by lightning and die before they can be taken to the hospital. A tornado strikes a town, devastates scores of buildings, and takes several lives.

We are all aware of events such as these – and tens of thousands more – in our neighborhood, our state, our nation, and around the world. Yes, *stuff happens*. And in some situations, they happen for an identifiable reason. But in others they just happen – without any reason or understanding of why they occurred as they did.

Are they part of a plan? Are they part of God's plan? Or, do they happen apart from any plan? Or, to put it more directly: Does God actually have a plan for everything that takes place in the world?

These questions lead us to the third means by which God expresses his character, namely, helping human beings understand what God is doing. To believe God has a precise plan for everything that happens makes God the one who determines what is going to take place. But if God has limited himself in proportion to the freedom God has given us, and if God does not control everything, then it is difficult – if not impossible – to affirm that God has a precise plan for every day-by-day activity.

It is misleading to say that God has a wonderful plan for our lives, if we mean, first, that God has a detailed plan for all that will take place in our lives, and, second, that our lives are going to be wonderful. We've already concluded that the first of these assumptions is inaccurate. The second needs clarification because many people don't have wonderful lives – at least not during certain periods of their lives. Think for a moment of the anguish and pain going on in some people's lives in your world – perhaps in your own life or that of your family or close friends. Think also about those in your community, your state, and the many places of incredible need throughout this country. And, if that is not enough, think about the people around the world – people living in horrendous situations of poverty, squalor, disease, violence, crime, and war.

And then stop . . . , and ask yourself if this is the plan God has for them – if this is the wonderful life that God wants for them. Perhaps such a question is unnecessary. Perhaps the answer is obvious. Nevertheless, it is important to think deeply about other people in the world who live in situations that may be quite different from our own.

Not only is it misleading to say that God has a wonderful plan for everyone's life, it is also misleading to claim that Jeremiah 29:11 supports the understanding that God has a plan for the details of our lives, and the lives of everyone else. The New Revised Standard Version translates this verse: "For surely I know the plans I have for you, says the Lord, plans for your welfare and not for harm, to give you a future with hope." The Hebrew word for "plans" is *machshavot* – plural, not singular – a term that can be translated "thoughts, devices, purposes, or plans," but is most commonly translated "thoughts."

A more accurate rendition of the Hebrew text is that given in *The Holy Scriptures,* a translation by the Jewish Publication Society of America: "For I know the thoughts that I think toward you, says the Lord, thoughts of peace, and not evil, to give you a future and a hope." God is expressing his supportive thoughts for Israel during a time of judgment, punishment, and suffering – a time of exile that Jeremiah says will last a lifetime.

What may be more understandable and more accurate than God having a detailed plan for your life, and everyone else's life, is to think of God having a purpose – a very promising and hopeful purpose – one that can be more meaningful than a specific plan! This is the overall premise of Rick Warren's books, *The Purpose Driven Life: What on Earth Am I Here For?* and his sequel, *Better Together: What on Earth Are We Here For?*

Thinking of God carrying out his activities with a purpose means God has goals God is attempting to achieve. However, human beings exercise their freedom and often frustrate what God is seeking to accomplish. Nevertheless, when such roadblocks arise, God is resolute in his purpose; that is, God is constantly working to bring it about, regardless of what circumstances arise – regardless of how people respond. Job, in his dialog with God, said it this way: "I know that no *purpose* of yours can be thwarted" (42:2). James, in his epistle (5:1), gives an affirmation of this understanding: "You have heard of the endurance of Job, and you have seen the *purpose* of the Lord, how the Lord is compassionate and merciful" (i.e., a God of steadfast love).

Although God doesn't have a wonderful "plan" for everyone's life, God does have a wonderful "purpose" for your life, and for everyone else's life – all around the world. And, as the writer of the epistle to the Hebrews puts it, God shows to the heirs of his promise "the unchange-able character of his *purpose*" (6:17). God has a purpose that remains resolute – doesn't change – even though his activity in carrying it out is influenced by the actions of you, me, and everyone else in the world.

Furthermore, to believe that God has a constant, ongoing purpose, but not a specific plan for everything that happens in life, doesn't mean God doesn't have an overall plan that will eventually work out at the end of history as we know it. God does have that type of plan. God will be victorious. God's reign – experienced only in part during this life – will one day come to fruition in all its fullness!

This understanding is similar to what we human beings experience every day on a smaller, less consequential scale. For example, we go on a trip by car, and when we get to a construction site, we see a sign that says "detour." Our overall plan changes – by necessity – and we find ourselves on other roads for a period of time. Nevertheless, our overall plan is the same and, eventually, we arrive at our destination, though we may be late.

Or, we begin planting shrubs and flowers outside a home we just purchased. We set out the plantings according to the plan that we have drawn on a piece of paper. However, as we dig the first hole, we find large roots are in our way. We move the shrub several feet away, and dig another hole. This time few roots obstruct us. We plant the shrub, and then turn to the sweeping corner of the garden, and set out the very large bush we bought for that location. However, as we start to dig, we encounter a stone – much too large to remove – at that precise location. We soon realize we have to widen the curve of the garden to accommodate this special bush. And so the process continues across the front of the house. Near the end of the day we look at what we've planted and celebrate how it looks, though some of the plants are not even close to the places we had planned when we started.

We could go on and on with illustrations such as applying for a particular job, not getting it, and having to find a different one; or, training for a position on a sports team, having an injury, and realizing that the tryout must wait for another year; or, planning to have minor surgery, but finding out surgery will be major and subsequent treatments will be extensive. Such illustrations help us understand that when we say God has an overall plan, we have to account for similar types of changes – numerous changes. And that complicates and at times even negates the idea that God has a precise plan for our day-by-day activities.

When we reflect on the word "purpose" and think about persons who feel compelled, constrained, driven by a purpose, we are describing those who have a goal – or a series of goals – governing their lives. Plans to accomplish that purpose can and will change as circumstances arise. This is what a sailor does when preparing to start a race. The goal is clear: winning the race. The strategy depends on what other boats are racing; the condition of the winds, waves, and currents; and what the sailor's boat is able to do best. The tactics are determined – in part – by what other boats do; by changes in wind direction and velocity; and by what opportunities arise that the sailor can take advantage of. But the sailor never loses sight of the goal: winning the race. An example of such an understanding is given by the writer of the Acts of the Apostles as he recounts the journey of Paul on his way to Rome: "When a moderate south wind began to blow, they thought they could achieve their *purpose*; so they weighed anchor and began to sail past Crete, close to the shore" (27:13-44).

And so it is with God – though far more complex than we can describe in a limited number of pages. In short, God has a purpose; God has a strategy for carrying out that purpose; and God has a variety of tactics, depending on what human beings are doing in response to what God is doing. The common phrase we use for such activity is "the will of God." And we can gain some clarity in our understanding if we distinguish between what God really wants, what God is willing to accept, and what God eventually accomplishes.

The first of these distinctions is what is desirable from God's point of view – what God hopes for – what we have already defined as the highest expression of what God wants. The second is what God is willing to accept now that God has given human beings the freedom to make choices. And the third is what God will still accomplish in spite of human choices that temporarily thwart what God really wants.

In his classic bestseller, *The Will of God,* Leslie Weatherhead refers to these three levels of understanding as God's intentional will, God's circumstantial will, and God's ultimate will. A more recent book that deals with the same principles, but extends their implications in a number of ways, is *Why? Making Sense of God's Will,* by Adam Hamilton.

These different ways of understanding God's will are important to grasp – whether you agree with them or not – because the declaration we may make that an event is God's will can be harmful in some situations, and helpful in others. Distinguishing between what God wants and what God permits is incredibly important!

WORKS

Many verbs describe God's activity. Do particular ones immediately come to mind? Does one stand out above the others?

(PAUSE TO REFLECT)

In the Bible, in our creedal formulations, and in our hymnals, some verbs show up quite often. Some are visual, creating images and pictures. Others exemplify energy and power. Still others evoke a sense of calm and peace.

Rather than survey a broad array of verbs, we will look at one verb as a prime example of God's activity, both within our individual lives, our lives in Christian community, and our lives in the global world. It is the verb "works" – a word that is synonymous with carrying out activities.

The psalmist thanks the Lord "for his steadfast love, for his wonderful *works* to humankind" – a phrase he repeats four times in Psalm 107 (verses 8, 15, 21, and 31). Note how he ties together God's character (steadfast love) with God's activity (wonderful works).

Numerous passages in the Bible clarify how God is at work in people's lives. In the letter to the church at Philippi Paul writes: "Therefore, my beloved, just as you have always obeyed me, not only in my presence, but much more now in my absence, *work* out your own salvation with fear and trembling; for it is God who is at *work* in you, enabling you both to will and to *work* for his good pleasure" (Philippians 2:12-13). Here Paul uses the verb "work" to exhort the

Philippians to "work out" their own salvation, not through their own efforts, but by recognizing that it is "God who is at work" in them.

The letter to the Ephesians contains a further explanation of God at work: "Now to him who by the power at *work* within us is able to accomplish abundantly far more than all we can ask or imagine, to him be glory in the church and in Christ Jesus to all generations, forever and ever" (Ephesians 3:20-21). Note the incredible affirmation, namely, that God is able to accomplish what "we can ask or imagine."

Is that what it says? No, it says "*all* we can ask or imagine."

Is that the entirety of what it says? No, it says *"more than all..."*

Is that the totality of what it says? No, it says *"far more than all..."*

Is that the finality of what it says? No, it says, God is able to accomplish *"abundantly far more than all we can ask or imagine."*

What an affirmation!

This promise delineates what God is able to do. But how does God do this? The text says it is "by the power at *work* within us" – not within "me." In other words, it is an affirmation of the community of believers, not individuals on their own – separate from the community. Such an emphasis is reinforced by the plural pronoun "you" (in the Greek text) rather than the singular pronoun "you." In the next verse of the text, the word "you" is plural: "I beg *you* to lead a life worthy of the calling to which *you* have been called" (4:1). Second-person pronouns are quite common in New Testament epistles.

This does not mean such verses do not apply to individuals. Of course they do, but these writers are thinking primarily of the community of believers – the audience they are addressing. Their use of a plural form of the second-person pronoun enriches the interpretation of the text. For example, when Paul says "your body is a temple of the Holy Spirit," he is referring to the Christian community at Corinth as a body, rather than the physical form of an individual person – though it could be applied in that way as well.

While examining the use of pronouns in biblical texts can be enlightening, many other angles of vision can also be worthwhile. One of these is the varying translations of the original language of a particular verse—as we will see in the next section.

FOR GOOD

For what does God work? If we say "for good," what do we mean? Is it limited to the "steadfast love" we have already identified? Is it some type of moral goodness that goes beyond that? Or, in this context, is it a more functional term?

(PAUSE TO REFLECT)

Perhaps a review of the way the word "good" is used in the first chapter of Genesis will provide insight for our understanding. In those verses the Hebrew word *tov* (in the Greek Septuagint *agathos*) appears seven times in the opening creation story (once on days 1, 4 and 5; twice on days 3 and 6; and omitted from the text on day 2, unless an expression from day 3 is considered part of day 2). In each instance the meaning seems to be the same, namely, that God saw that the creation fulfilled the purpose God had in mind. This is the root meaning of *tov* – a functional term in these as well as other instances.

The writer summarizes this usage in verse 31: "God saw everything that God had made, and indeed, it was very *good*." God gave a word of approval to what God saw because all of creation fulfilled the purpose God had in mind. And such an understanding of good enables us to grasp more clearly what Paul had in mind when he wrote his letter to the church in Rome.

In Romans 8:28 the opening part of the verse is translated in the Revised Standard Version (RSV) in these words: "We know that *in everything God works for good*." The same basic wording also appears in the New International Version (NIV).

However, in the King James Version (KJV) the translation says: "We know that *all things work together for good*." We find the same wording in the New Revised Standard Version (NRSV).

The differences in these translations are important to understand. For we can easily misunderstand the meaning of this crucial passage. In the original Greek there is a present tense verb in third person, singular form (*sunergei*). It literally means "he works with." There is also a word (*panta*) that precedes the verb. It means "all," or "everything," and can function as the subject or the object of the verb (word order in Greek is often not significant).

The subject of the verb is clarified when the textual families behind the two translations are examined. One group of manuscripts has the verb without a subject other than the word "all." The other group has the word "God" (*Theos*) before it, with the definite article "the" (*o*), thereby making God the subject of the verb. And this reading comes from some highly regarded manuscripts, one of which is a papyrus dated from the late second or early third century (p46) – probably the earliest manuscript we have on this verse.

The point is this: The subject of the verb is "God" and not "all." This means "God works for good," not "all things work together for good." While the latter translation can be understood in the same way as the first translation, it sometimes is not. And here is where misunderstanding may arise. For if we interpret the verse to mean that all things work together – regardless of what they are – we can falsely assume that God is not the one who is at work to bring about good. Furthermore, if someone uses this translation to claim all things are somehow determined and controlled by God, we have another false assumption.

A second part to this verse is less significant for our interpretation, but can also be misunderstood: "*God works for good in everything*, with those who love God, who are called according to his *purpose*" (Romans 8:28). To claim that God only works for good with those who love God, is to interpret the text in a limited manner – one that is likely to become self-serving in scope. It may be easier and simpler for God to work for good when dealing with those who love God, but the text gives no indication that God is excluding others whom he loves, even though they may not express love to God.

God doesn't *cause* tragedy to happen so God can bring good out of it. No! God works in and through tragedy so God can accomplish his purpose even in the midst of tragedy. As we know all too well, *stuff happens* in life. Suffering, heartache, and anguish take place all too often. Yet God is always present – regardless of what may occur – seeking to bring about good.

Whatever happens in life, and however painful it may be, we can depend on God being good at that very moment, and at every moment thereafter. Nothing can take place that will destroy that goodness, and nothing can take place that will prevent God from working for good. That is, God will *always* be a God of steadfast love, and God will *always* express that steadfast love – regardless of what happens – regardless of what we may do or not do – regardless of what others may do or not do. Simply put: "Regardless!"

God is at work in our personal world. However, that is not all. God is also very much at work in the global world – every day, in every place, in every way – seeking to bring about good. In so doing, God looks for individuals and groups who will join him in such a venture – one that can become meaningful, sometimes exciting, and yet often incredibly painful. For, when persons become aware of what God is seeking to do, they can actually participate in what God is doing. Though this may sound presumptuous, it is not, especially if it is carried out in a spirit of deep humility – one that senses and acknowledges the profound privilege it is to share in such an undertaking.

To make this point as realistic and practical as possible, try to picture this scene in your mind: A woman is sitting and watching the evening news – filled with one tragedy after another – on her TV. As she does this she prays, "God, I believe you are working for good in the midst of all this tragedy." She watches some more. Then she prays again: "Help me, God, to understand how you are working in these situations." She continues watching. Then she prays once again, "Help me, God, to find some way to participate with you in your work."

Think, for a moment about the steps this woman is taking as she seeks to become a participant. She begins by stating her belief. She continues by asking for understanding. She concludes by making a request for assistance to find a way to participate in God's work.

Are there any exceptions? When people say, "all the time," do they mean it in a literal sense? When the server at the Italian restaurant says, "Yes, there is garlic in everything," is he including drinks and desserts? When a director of an improvisational theater speaks about a talented actress and says, "That woman is so versatile; she's in everything," does he really mean she's in every dramatic sketch?

In situations such as these – when people use the words "in everything" – do they literally mean what they are saying? Or, are they merely expressing an overstatement to share a sentiment? If we quizzed them about such statements, perhaps they would say, "Well, you know what I mean." And we would.

However, when it comes to the claim this chapter is making, namely, that God works for good in everything, is it the same as the common meaning of the words "in everything?" Is God literally working for good at all times and in all places?

(PAUSE TO REFLECT)

During those times that are filled to capacity with joy and celebration, we can recognize God easily – if one is open to such recognition. Even during the times filled with such feelings to a lesser degree, we can still recognize God. But when such feelings are almost gone, so does the recognition of God fade. And when those feelings are not present at all, the recognition of God is often lost.

However, during any one of those times, God is still present and still working for good. It may not be noticeable at all. Or, it may barely be discernible. Nevertheless, God is still at work. You might, therefore, rightly ask about the extent of God's activity. Does it pertain to everything in our lives – every little thing? Or, do we need to modify our understanding so that we think about the things related to God's *purpose* in our lives, in the world in which we live, and in the global world of which we are a part?

This is important to consider when we use the words "in everything." We don't participate with God, and expect God to participate with us in the trivia of our lives – those things that may seem important to us, but can't be justified as important to God: finding an empty space in a crowded parking lot; locating a particular item at the mall; calling another store to get the right size for an article of clothing. Matters such as these are not very high on God's list of activities – if indeed they are even on his list. God is concerned with carrying out his purpose in the world, not in being used for the fulfillment of trivial desire.

You may be asking yourself how such a truth – **God works for good in everything** – can make itself known in a person's life. Here's an illustration from a real-life situation:

Chuck, age forty-four, was the father of two boys—Jake (twelve) and Travis (nine)—and was living the life he had always hoped he would: wonderful wife and mother, two great sons, excellent job, meaningful relationship with God, and active in his church as well as his community.

What happened late one Saturday afternoon was as far from his mind as the moon is from the earth, but it did happen at a railroad crossing in Indiana. The two boys were riding with another family in a SUV that didn't make it across the tracks before a train slammed into it. Jake was pronounced dead at the scene; Travis died in the hospital hours later.

Words cannot describe the shock and anguish that Chuck and his wife, Becky, felt! It was almost unbearable! And if it had not been for their faith in God through Jesus Christ, they might never have worked through such a ghastly ordeal!

As days and weeks went by, Chuck decided to share his faith with others—including interviews with the media—that God is present in the most devastating circumstances on earth! His capacity to do this with a high degree of effectiveness grew out of the incredible support and encouragement he received from his family and friends, especially his pastors and fellow church members.

One of the developments that emerged rapidly was the establishment of a fund for the upgrading of the railroad crossing at the location where the accident happened. It became known as the "Jake and Travis Arms of Life Fund." Within nine months sufficient funds were raised to construct this new crossing, including large moving arms and flashing lights. Not only that, but enough contributions poured in to build crossings at three additional locations in the area.

Another response to this tragedy was the special recognition Jake and Travis received from their fellow students, teachers, and administrators at the school they attended. A special award called "The Findley Award for Excellence" was established in memory of the outstanding qualities demonstrated by each of the boys. It is awarded each year to the student who exemplifies these qualities most fully.

A third response came from Tony Dungy, coach of the Indianapolis Colts, when he returned to the city the day after the Super Bowl victory. While reading the newspaper, he saw the headline of the accident just below the headline of the championship. Having lost a son himself, Tony was immediately drawn to the story. But it was not until some weeks later, when he accepted an invitation to come and help Travis' classmates deal with their loss, that Tony would meet Chuck. And what a meaningful time that was! And what a significant relationship that initiated!

Still another development took place when Chuck became aware of a group of fathers who were meeting in a coffee shop every Tuesday morning at 7:00 am to share what life was like after the loss of a son or a daughter. He became a part of this group and found it so valuable that he later referred to it as one of the most important decisions of his life. (His story, along with stories of 13 other dads, is included in the book, **Tuesday Mornings with the Dads: Stories by Fathers Who Have Lost a Son or a Daughter**.)

Looking back at these developments, and others that have taken place since his sons died, Chuck said: "I realize God has been at work, seeking to bring good out of the tragic death of my sons, Jake and Travis. I also realize I need to cooperate with God in making this happen!"

PARTICIPATING IN IT

QUESTIONS

Responding to the following questions is one means of comprehending this truth more fully, and thereby participating in it more completely.

First, review what you've read (as well as recalling your answers to the questions at the end of chapter 1):

- What is the writer's understanding of the words – "God" – "works" – "for good" – "in everything" – in this chapter?
- To what extent do you agree or disagree with this understanding?

Second, relate what you've read to your own life:

- How would you put your understanding into your own words?
- What feelings would you associate with your understanding?
- In what ways have you already participated in this truth?
- How do you think you will participate in this truth in the months and years to come?

Third, connect your understanding, your feelings, your participation, and your expectations regarding this truth with others – individually or in a group.

Formulating your own questions is another means – perhaps a more effective one.

Reflecting on the questions you've formulated and discussing them with others is still another possibility.

PRACTICES

There are various ways to express truth #2 verbally, whether in church, at home, or some other setting in the community:

Memorize it as a single sentence, or two separate phrases.

Recite the sentence by itself, or each phrase as a call and response. (Consider saying it responsively at a dinner during Lent, perhaps your Easter dinner – if you have one – or at another time that may be more suitable.)

Write out for yourself what the truth means to you, including examples of how you understand it (in your heart and in your head), as well as how it has become a part of your life.

Share with someone else what you think it means, how it makes you feel, and ways it has become a part of your life. (Consider sharing with the same group.)

Have someone else – either an individual or a group – **share** with you and others what they think it means, how it makes them feel, and how they have participated in it. (Consider inviting others from the same group to share.)

Utilize it in your everyday activities, whether you meditate on it, say it aloud to a family member or friend, or mention it in a group setting.

PRAYERS

Making use of the following words is one manner of praying:

Gracious God, we thank you that
   you work for good,
   with those who love you, and
   with those who do not.
Loving God, we thank you that
   you work for good in everything,
   when life is going reasonably well, and
   when life is going horribly wrong.
Help us, O God, to participate in your work
   as we think about it,
   as we talk about it with you and with others, and

as we show it in our lives . . . in everything we do.

Through Jesus Christ we pray. Amen.

Composing a prayer in your own words is another method – perhaps even a more meaningful one.

MUSIC – *as found on the next page*

There are various ways to express truth #2 musically – either in unison or in rounds – whether it is in church, at home, or in some other setting in the community:

Sing it by yourself or in a group.
(Consider inviting the same group to join in singing.)

Hum it by yourself or in a group.

Teach others to sing and/or hum it.

Record it, or have it recorded by someone else, and then play it for others to hear.

God Works for Good, in Everything

God works for good, God works for good, in ev - ery - thing. In ev - ery - thing, in ev - ery - thing, God works for good.

* May be sung to a round in three groups.

Words: Adolf Hansen
Music: Folk Melody
© 2002 Adolf Hansen

CHAPTER 3

TRUST GOD, NO MATTER WHAT

NO MATTER WHAT, TRUST GOD

INVITATION OF GOD

"Trust in God with all your heart,
and do not rely on your own insight."

Proverbs 3:5

The "third simple truth" is not expressed in many circles across the theological spectrum in the precise wording utilized in this volume. However, the verse that is the basis for it is one of the most well known verses among Evangelicals, Moderates, and Progressives. Nevertheless, believers rarely recite it in a responsive manner in which the leader begins by saying, "Trust God," with the congregation responding, "no matter what," followed by the leader repeating the words, "no matter what," and the congregation responding, "Trust God."

This truth has only five words, rather than six (since the subject "you" is implicit): a verb (trust), an object (God), and a categorical phrase (no matter what).

The way these words relate to circumstances in life may vary, but the core meaning is commonly accepted, especially the first two words. The last three words comprise one of a variety of expressions that attempt to be as inclusive as possible: "regardless," or "come what may," or "nonetheless," or "in any case."

TRUST

In chapters one and two you were asked what you thought about when you heard the word "God." In this chapter we continue thinking about God, but we begin with the word "trust." What does that word bring to mind? What feelings does it evoke?

(PAUSE TO REFLECT)

Trust is a part of our everyday experience. We trust operators of cars and trucks to drive responsibly – obey traffic signals, stay in their lanes (unless they intentionally make a change), and avoid accidents. We trust the food we eat and the water we drink. We trust doctors, nurses, and other medical staff. We trust pastors and rabbis, parents and spouses, family and friends. When we think about it, we realize life necessitates a considerable amount of trust. At the same time, we also recognize that all circumstances are open to betrayal.

We can never guarantee trust. If we try to do that, we destroy the core of its meaning. Trust is a quality of life we begin to learn, or not learn, soon after we are born. An infant often learns to trust the consistency of a primary caregiver and, if that environment maintains itself, he or she learns to trust himself or herself.

Trust is the basis for all stages of development throughout our lives if we are going to become mature, emotionally healthy adults. This means trust is foundational for each and every stage in life (a vertical perspective), as well as essential for all subsequent stages to come to full maturity (a horizontal perspective).

If we are going to learn to trust others, we must begin by trusting ourselves. It is an understanding that is paralleled by what Jesus said in the two great commandments: "Love God with all your heart, soul, mind, and strength" (a quotation from Deuteronomy 6:4-5, with the addition of the word "mind" in Matthew, Mark, and Luke); and "Love your neighbor as yourself" (a quotation from Leviticus 19:18).

You might wonder what the parallel is between the word "love" and the word "trust." Love has many nuances of meaning, one of which is trust. When speaking of people, we commonly think of trust as part of love. However true that is, there is another point that may even be more significant, namely, the words "as you love yourself." These words evince an assumption that we need to love ourselves in order to love others. In like manner, to trust others we need to trust ourselves.

There isn't any necessary sequence between trusting ourselves and trusting others. One doesn't have to come before the other, though sometimes one leads the way. At other times both take place simultaneously. This means we may be limited in trusting others if we are limited in trusting ourselves. Conversely, it also means we can deeply trust others if we deeply trust ourselves. It's an ongoing interactive process: trusting ourselves more fully may lead us to do the same with others. And, vice versa, trusting others more fully may lead us to do the same with ourselves.

When parents of a young boy living on a farm give him permission to take the tractor for a ride by himself, they trust him and he trusts himself. When the parents of a young girl living in a small town allow their daughter to ride a bicycle by herself to a friend's house several blocks away, they trust her and she trusts herself. If the children didn't trust themselves to be able to go for a ride, they might not go. Furthermore, if the parents didn't trust their children, the parents might indicate that their children would need to wait till they got a little older.

Such an understanding focuses on "trust of oneself" and "trust of others toward oneself." However, there is also "trust of others by oneself." This means we have to trust others as well as have others trust us. And when we do this, we are experiencing faith, security, confidence, reliance, dependence, assurance, and hope. And the way we do this exemplifies a relationship that is mutual. Both of the individuals in the relationship trust each other.

Most of us have relationships of mutual trust. And many of us have a number of them, though they may vary in degree – some very deep, others moderately deep, and still others not very deep at all. Furthermore, most of us have some relationships where trust is barely present – if at all.

Think about your life. Who comes to mind in each of these four categories? Are there some persons in each of them? How would you describe these varying relationships? What feelings, as well as what thoughts do they evoke? What are the qualities that make some of these relationships so meaningful?

Think also about the betrayals of trust you have experienced. How would you describe them? What led up to them? How did you handle them? What did you learn from them?

Relationships of trust can be incredibly meaningful. Yet they can also be incredibly painful, whether you have been betrayed or you have betrayed someone else. And the work that is needed takes time – sometimes a great deal of time – to restore the relationship to the previous depths known before the betrayal, if indeed that depth can ever be reached again.

Some individuals have been hurt so deeply that they have great difficulty in ever coming to deeply trust an individual again. That's sad, but true. And such individuals need considerable understanding as well as highly competent intervention to learn to trust again. For example, when a woman came to her pastor and said she wasn't experiencing a trust relationship with God, but was yearning to know what she needed to do to find it, her pastor asked her to think about the person she trusted most in this life. This was difficult for her and very painful. Tears began to well up in her eyes – tears that slowly ran down her cheeks. Finally she said, "I don't have anyone I can really trust." Silence permeated the room. Slowly she wiped her eyes, looked up and said, "I think I need to work on developing a trust relationship with one or two of my friends. Maybe that will help me to find a trust relationship with God."

When we reflect on trust, we are examining the core dimension of our lives – one that connects us to a deep and profound experience of trust with God. However, that is not all. For what we experience with God is directly related to what we experience with others. The writer of the epistle of First John puts it this way: "Those who say 'I love God,' and hate their brothers and sisters, are liars; for those who do not love a brother or sister whom they have seen, cannot love God whom they have not seen" (1 John 4:20). Replacing the word "love" with the word "trust" – one of the dimensions of love – leads us to express it this way: "Those who say 'I trust God,' and mistrust their brothers or sisters . . . whom they have seen, cannot trust God whom they have not seen."

Trust in ourselves is very important. So is the trust we receive from others. And so is the trust we extend to others. But even more profound than each of these is the trust we extend to God, and the trust we receive from God!

GOD

Is there one image of God that stands out the most when you think of putting your trust in God? If so, what is that image? How did it get started in your life? How did it develop? How would you describe it at this point in your life? Is the image comforting, disturbing, or a mixture of the two?

(PAUSE TO REFLECT)

The understanding of God that we've used in this discussion has focused on one who shows steadfast love to us – and to all human beings – one who invites us to trust him. A psalmist puts it this way: "*Steadfast love* surrounds those who *trust* in the Lord" (32:10). Note that he uses a verb signifying an all-encompassing scope and an ongoing, continuous activity. What he is describing is not simply an isolated event at a given point in time. It's a daily way of life. Other psalmists express this assurance in personal statements. One declares: "I *trust* in your *steadfast love*" (13:5); another prays: "Let me hear of your *steadfast love* in the morning, for in you I put my *trust*" (143:8); and, as if this wasn't enough, another says: "I *trust* in the *steadfast love* of God for ever and ever" (52:8).

In numerous passages in the Old Testament the hearers are invited – even urged – to "trust in the Lord." In one Psalm, this phrase is repeated three times, each followed by the words: "He is their help and their shield" (Psalm 115:9, 10, 11). In another Psalm, the results are even more specific: "O Most High, when I am afraid, I put my *trust* in you. In God, whose word I praise, in God I *trust*; I am not afraid; what can flesh do to me?" (Psalm 56:3-4, as well as 56:11). Likewise, the writer of Isaiah declares: "Surely God is my salvation; I will *trust,* and will not be afraid, for the Lord God is my strength and my might" (Isaiah 12:2). In short, for those people at that time, and for us today, we don't have to be afraid if we put our trust in God!

The Hebrew word for "trust" in these passages is *batach* – a word that appears 120 times in the Old Testament, 46 of which are in the Psalms. While there are various nuances of meaning in the respective contexts in which this word is used, the basic understanding is essentially the same when it refers to God. The focus is on a relationship that human beings can have with God, the one who expresses himself – at all times and in all places – as steadfast love.

When the word "trust" describes that relationship, the emphasis is on a response to an invitation from God, the one who takes the initiative to reach out to us and to all humans. Words that define that response more fully are found in such verbs as "rely on" – "have confidence in" – "feel secure."

These verbs are built on a foundation of firmness, solidarity, dependability – yes, trustworthiness. This means human beings in general, and we in particular, can experience the meaning of these words in our lives. We can rely on God; we can have confidence in God; and we can feel secure, because we have a relationship that is firm, solid, dependable, and trustworthy. What an incredible invitation God extends to us!

However, that is not all. Trust is not a one-way street. Trust is mutual. This means that God also wants to trust us. God wants to rely on us, have confidence in us, and feel secure with us. God wants to have a relationship with us that's firm, solid, dependable – yes, trustworthy. What a privilege! And what a responsibility!

We are invited to trust God who, in turn, is willing to trust us. Is this what we're saying? Not quite, for God is not only willing to trust us, God is also putting that willingness into practice. God trusts us to carry out God's work in the world. What trust God is placing in us!

It is with a profound sense of humility that we dare to believe that this is true. But that's the nature of trust. It's mutual, just like trust relationships you have with other human beings. Think for a moment of the person you trust the most. Isn't it reciprocal? How else would you have a trust relationship, unless you trusted one another? Yes, one of you might have a deeper level of trust toward the other. But, trust has to be present in both directions. How profound this is when we think about the trust God has in us – a trust that is far more profound than the trust we have in God!

Yet, the trust God has in us can be unrealized – that is, never understood. Or, it can be understood, but forgotten. Or, it can be betrayed. How God must grieve over human beings – yes, us as well – when we forget God is yearning to trust us, or when we betray the trust God has in us.

At those times, and at all times, we need to remember that God's character is good, all the time; that God's activity is to work for good, in everything. And the God we describe in this manner will continue to be good, and to work for good, regardless of how we respond, regardless of how we ignore or reject God's invitation to trust.

It is very interesting that the Septuagint (the Greek translation of the Hebrew Bible that Paul and other leaders of the early Church used) does not use the verb we might expect in translating the Hebrew word "trust" (*batach*), namely, the verb "believe" (*pisteuo*). Instead, the Septuagint uses the word "hope" (*elpizo*).

What this means is that the translators of the Septuagint didn't want to translate "trust" in a way that would lose an experiential reliance on God. They didn't want to use a word that would be – or at least might be – understood as an intellectual response to God. They wanted to communicate the profound meaning of "trust" (*batach*) – one that would emphasize the feeling of being safe and secure.

The relationship of "trust" and "hope" is interesting at many levels. One is simply the translation of the Hebrew word into Greek (as we have noted). Another is the understanding of hope as trust in the future. Trust in the present may not be sufficient. Trust may also need to look ahead. Likewise, being able to hope may enable us to trust. These are profound connections: trust enabling hope, and hope enabling trust. No wonder the translators of the Septuagint chose the verb "hope" rather than the verb "believe."

One of the psalmists makes the connection explicit in a personal word of witness: "For you, O Lord, are my *hope*, my *trust*, O Lord, from my youth. Upon you I have leaned from my birth; it was you who took me from my mother's womb. My praise is continually of you" (71:5-6). Another psalmist links these two words in a communal declaration of faith: "Our soul waits for the Lord; he is our help and shield. Our heart is glad in him, because we *trust* in his holy name. Let your *steadfast love*, O Lord, be upon us, even as we *hope* in you" (33:20-22).

It is interesting that the Greek language does not have a word that distinctively means "trust," in the way the Hebrew language does. The verb "believe" (*pisteuo*, as well as compound forms such as *empisteuo*) may express trust as acceptance of another's claim, but such an understanding was not central to the translators of the Septuagint. As a result, the New Testament does not speak explicitly about "trust." Instead, the word "faith" (*pistis*) is used – over and over again – in the Synoptic Gospels (Matthew, Mark, and Luke), and is sometimes paired with the Greek verb that means "to save, to heal, to make whole" (*sozo*). The affirmation is then translated, "your faith has saved you," or "your faith has healed you," or "your faith has made you whole" – all accurate translations of the same Greek words.

The word "faith" is never used in the Fourth Gospel (John). Instead the verb "believe" occurs repeatedly (98 times), while the noun "belief" does not occur. For example, the writer says: "Jesus did many other signs in the presence of his disciples, which are not written in this book. But these are written so that you may come to *believe* that Jesus is the Messiah, the Son of God, and that through *believing* you may have life in his name" (20:31). Note that "believing" is the means to new life – an experiential matter, not simply an intellectual assent.

In addition to the limited capacity to translate *batach* directly into Greek, and its consequent lack of explicit use in the New Testament, this verb is rarely used in documents written in the Hebrew language outside the Old Testament. Nevertheless, the use of the word "trust" (in English and other modern languages) has been significant. For it permeates Christian communities around the world.

The word "trust" shows up in numerous hymns. Besides the familiar ones – "Only Trust Him" (UMH, 337) and "Trust and Obey" (UMH, 467) – there are hymns such as "Through It All" (UMH, 507), with its central message in the expression, "I've learned to trust in Jesus, I've learned to trust in God." Note the interchangeability of the one to whom trust is expressed – "Jesus" and "God" – another clear affirmation of the triune Godhead. Likewise note the two hymns with virtually identical titles, "My God, I Love Thee" (UMH, 476) and "My Jesus, I Love Thee" (UMH, 172). Note also the well-known hymn, "Tis So Sweet to Trust in Jesus" (UMH, 462) – a hymn that includes the words, "I'm so glad I learned to trust thee, precious Jesus, Savior, friend," as well as, "O for grace to trust him more."

Affirmations of trust in God, or trust in Jesus, are common in preaching, worship, and study of the Bible, as well as in music. Various biblical passages are the basis for this, even when the word "trust" isn't explicitly used in the English translation of the Greek text. For example, the writer of the fourth Gospel uses the verb "believe" in one verse (14:1) where "believe" is sometimes translated "trust," in order for the reader to grasp the full meaning of the passage. Following the words, "Do not let your hearts be troubled," the text says, "Believe in God, believe also in me." They could also be translated: "Trust in God, trust also in me." A fuller significance of this verse, however, is that the affirmation states the same phrase twice – first using the words "in God," and then using the words "in me" (referring to Jesus as the one who is speaking these words).

What makes this so powerful is that Jesus set the example for us to follow. He trusted God to such an extent that he surrendered his life – his will – when he said: "Father, if you are willing, remove this cup from me; yet, not my will but yours be done" (Luke 22:42). We express these same words in the Lord's Prayer when we say: "Your name be hallowed; your kingdom come; your will be done."

Yet Jesus is more than an example – as significant as that is. He did show us how to deal with suffering when he was betrayed, shamed, tortured, and nailed to a cross. But he also came to show us what God is like. This means God is like Jesus. For Jesus was *God manifest in the flesh!*

In addition, he died for us and for all human beings – died for our sins and the sins of the whole world. Still further, God raised Jesus from the dead so that we, and all human beings, might experience a personal relationship with the risen Christ – one that is so close that New Testament writers speak of followers of Jesus being "in Christ" and having "Christ in them" (e.g., Colossians 1:2, 27). Such a relationship is more than following an example. It is a relationship that involves acceptance, forgiveness, and trust in God the Father, the risen Christ, and the Holy Spirit!

Affirmations of the triune Godhead are common throughout the

New Testament as well as the history of the Christian Church. However, this does not mean that a trust relationship with God is limited to those persons who believe in a triune Godhead. Such a relationship is also a possibility for our brothers and sisters of the Jewish faith, as well as those who express their faith in a Unitarian manner. These groups affirm God's character and God's activity in a manner that utilizes some of the same passages of the Bible as those that this book has referenced. Furthermore, persons in other faiths – as well as outside of identifiable faiths – receive an invitation from God to experience a trust relationship with him.

NO MATTER WHAT

What comes to mind when you hear the words "no matter what?" Do they mean "most of the time?" Do they literally mean "all of the time?" Do they leave any room for exceptions?

(PAUSE TO REFLECT)

The most explicit biblical reference to this section of the chapter comes from one of the Psalms: "Trust God *at all times*, O people; pour out your heart before him. God is a refuge for us" (62:8). This expression pertains not only to common, ordinary, routine times, but also to times of great celebration such as the birth of a healthy baby, the wedding of a wonderful couple, the incredible promotion at work, the victory of a highly prized athletic event, the achievement of a very significant goal, etc. Some people enjoy such celebrations.

However, many other people experience times of almost indescribable devastation such as the birth of a seriously challenged or stillborn child; an intense struggle with addiction; verbally/emotionally/ mentally/physically abusive relationships; poverty that makes daily existence/survival almost impossible; illness that involves excruciating pain/incapacity to function/early death; the destruction of lives and property through explosion/typhoon/war; the murder of innocent lives; the death of those who mean the most to us.

It may be relatively easy to trust God in good times, even the common, ordinary, routine times. But to trust God in the midst of horrendous times – often too gruesome to put into words – is another matter. Is it even possible to trust God in such circumstances? When God could intervene, but doesn't, why should we trust God? Why not just be angry with God, or even curse God?

These are significant questions, especially when a person – or a group of persons – is immersed in a ghastly, horrific experience. Where is God when such an experience takes place? And why should we trust God when this is our experience?

Although words may not be as helpful as a hug or an active listening ear, there are thoughts we might apply to our own lives, and – if appropriate – share with others, especially those going through difficult times. Sometimes a starting point might be one or more of the truths set forth in the preceding pages.

If it is true that God is good all the time, and if it is true that God is working to bring about good in every situation, we can trust God – regardless of what is taking place. God will never betray his own character. God will never betray the activities that express his character.

The writer of the Proverbs says it this way: "Trust God with all your heart, and do not rely on your own insight" (Proverbs 3:5). He encourages readers of his day, as well as readers of our day, to trust God with all of our being. This means we are invited to trust God, no matter what takes place. Furthermore, we are reminded not to regard our insight as necessarily sufficient, because sometimes it will not be.

Although a lot of things happen in life that we don't fully comprehend, we can still experience God in the midst of them, particularly when life's situations are teeming with pain. God is always there. That's how God expresses his power. That's what God has promised – *always* to be present to show his steadfast love, especially in the midst of our pain. God hurts with us. God anguishes with us. God cries with us. That's the most meaningful understanding of God's power – *the power of presence!*

In Paul's letter to the church at Corinth, he encourages them in their "trial" – a Greek word (*peirasmos*) that is also included in the Lord's Prayer, and can be translated as either "temptation" or "trial." He writes: "No trial has overtaken you that is not common to everyone. God is faithful, and he will not let you be tested beyond your strength, but with the testing he will also provide a way out so that you may be able to endure it" (1 Corinthians 10:13). This doesn't mean "God won't give you more than you can handle," because God is not the cause of the trial. *Stuff simply happens!* It does mean God is the one who is faithful and will provide a way for us to endure the time of testing, however painful and difficult that might be. Therefore we can *trust God, no matter what!*

In another passage to the same community of believers, Paul once again encourages them by saying: "We are afflicted in every way, but not crushed; perplexed, but not driven to despair; persecuted, but not forsaken; struck down, but not destroyed" (2 Corinthians 4:8-9). In the translation of J. B. Phillips: "Knocked down, but not knocked out."

Trusting God regardless of what happens in this life is, however, not the final message. Isaiah, as well as others, declares: "Trust in the Lord forever." Trust God not only in this life, but also in death. A well-known hymn, "Jesus Is All the World to Me" (UMH, 469), sets forth this same understanding: "I trust him now, I'll trust him when life's fleeting days shall end." Another hymn, "I Will Trust in the Lord" (UMH, 464), echoes the same word of witness: "I will trust in the Lord, till I die."

Whether you are younger or older in years, whether you are going through a joyful or sad time in life, whether you are well or sick, whether you are new to the faith or have had a meaningful relationship with God for many years, whether you have many friends or only a few, whether you feel you belong or not, you are invited to trust God.

You may be contemplating how such a truth – **Trust God, No Matter What** – can be embodied in a person's life. Here's an illustration from a real-life situation:

Jon, age 9, and his family were active in a church in a small town in Ohio. Like most boys his age, he loved athletics, especially soccer. His enthusiasm was evident as he played on a team in a community league.

During a game when he was dribbling the ball up the field, he and another player from the opposing team collided. Jon took a nasty fall and severely injured his left arm.

After an exam at the emergency room, it became clear that Jon had fractured a bone—in two places—in his left forearm. Some immediate treatment was given, but surgery had to wait until the swelling went down.

One morning a few days later, the youth pastor from his church stopped by Jon's hospital room prior to his going into surgery. After a conversation with him and his mother, a brief word of prayer, and a word of reassurance, Jon looked directly at his pastor and said, "I'm gonna trust God, no matter what!" He had learned it in church school, was able to internalize it in his life, and could now express it as his affirmation. He really got it!

RESPONDING TO IT

QUESTIONS

Responding to the following questions is one means of understanding this truth more fully.

First, review what you've read (as well as your answers to the questions at the end of chapters 1 and 2):

- What is the writer's understanding of the words – "trust" – "God" – "no matter what" – in this chapter?
- To what extent do you agree or disagree with this understanding?

Second, relate what you've read to your own life:

- How would you put your understanding into your own words?
- What feelings would you associate with your understanding?
- In what ways have you already responded to this truth?
- How do you think you will respond to this truth in the months and years to come?

Third, connect your understanding, your feelings, your responses, and your expectations regarding this truth with others—individually or in a group.

Formulating your own questions is another means – perhaps a more effective one.

Reflecting on the questions you've formulated and discussing them with others is still another possibility.

PRACTICES

There are various ways to express truth #3 verbally, whether in church, at home, or some other setting in the community:

Memorize it as a single sentence, or two separate phrases.

Recite the sentence by itself, or each phrase as a call and response. (Consider saying it responsively at a dinner during ordinary time, perhaps your Thanksgiving dinner – if you have one – or at another time that may be more suitable.)

Write out for yourself what the truth means to you, including examples of how you understand it (in your heart and in your head), as well as how it has become a part of your life.

Share with someone else what you think it means, how it makes you feel, and ways it has become a part of your life. (Consider sharing with the same group.)

Have someone else – either an individual or a group – **share** with you and others what they think it means, how it makes them feel, and how they have responded to it. (Consider inviting others from the same group to share.)

Utilize it in your everyday activities, whether you meditate on it, say it aloud to a family member or friend, or mention it in a group setting.

PRAYERS

Making use of the following words is one manner of praying:

Gracious God, we thank you that

> we can trust you with all our heart,
>
> that we can use our understanding,
>
> though we cannot always rely on it.

Loving God, we thank you that

> we can trust you, no matter what,
>
> when life is going reasonably well, and
>
> when life is going horribly wrong.

Help us, O God, to accept your invitation to trust you with all our heart,

> as we think about it,

as we talk about it with you and with others, and

as we embody it in our lives . . . no matter what.

Through Jesus Christ we pray. Amen.

Composing a prayer in your own words is another method – perhaps even a more meaningful one.

M U S I C – *as found on the next page*

There are various ways to express truth #3 musically – either in unison or in harmony – whether it is in church, at home, or in some other setting in the community:

Sing it by yourself or in a group.

(Consider inviting the same group to join in the singing.)

Hum it by yourself or in a group.

Teach others to sing and/or hum it.

Record it, or have it recorded by someone else and then play it for others to hear.

Trust God, No Matter What

Words: Anon
Music: Anon., arr. Adolf Hansen
© 2013 Adolf Hansen

Postscript: Experiencing These Truths

LOOKING BACK

Since the subtitle of the book speaks about experiencing these truths in our lives, I'd like to conclude by describing a few times in my life when these truths became very real, individually and in their interactions with each other.

CHILDHOOD

Life without a momentous crisis – experiencing all three truths

It began in the home where I grew up—an apartment in a working-class neighborhood. My parents were immigrants from Norway, having met each other as young adults in a church in Brooklyn, New York. Neither could speak English very well; neither had family in this country; neither had gone to high school; and neither had any money.

But what they did have was an emerging trust relationship with each other that brought together their respective trust relationships with God. And the context in which they nurtured these relationships, and developed new ones, was their new community of faith.

I was born into that household after they were married and had earned sufficient funds to start a family – my father as a carpenter and my mother as a nanny. From the beginning I learned to trust my parents. That was not difficult, for they were caring, thoughtful, and dependable. Their love was constant. It was never questioned; it was always there. As a result, I trusted them very deeply.

I discovered quite early that my parents had a deep trust relationship with God. They showed it to me in the way they lived, though I didn't consciously realize it until years later. The way they talked, the way each of them prayed aloud, the way they went to church so consistently, and the way they helped others, exuded a very real trust in God. As a result, I trusted God even before I realized that this is what I was doing.

As time went on I increasingly realized my parents weren't perfect, but they were good and diligently tried to bring about good. When they taught me about God, they repeatedly told me that God was the one who was good all the time, and that God was the one who worked for good in everything – not in those exact words, but with that same meaning.

Numerous problems arose during my childhood years, yet none was severe enough to threaten my trust relationship with God. It remained solid. But those years of life without a momentous crisis would soon come to an end.

COLLEGE YEARS

A crisis of faith and reason – struggling with truths #1 and #3

It took place during my junior year in college. I had just finished reading Paul Tillich's *Systematic Theology* and was trying to write a paper on his point of view, when I began to sense a penetrating conflict with my experience of God. If, as Tillich asserted, God was not a personal being (as I had come to experience God), but was "the ground of my being," or "being itself," then perhaps I'd been fooling myself.

In the middle of this intellectual struggle, I found it difficult to maintain my prayer life. How could I pray to the ground of my being? How could I worship being itself? I thought long and hard – day after day – and it wasn't helping my paper to get done; neither was it helping my prayer life. I was in such turmoil that I couldn't write the paper, and I couldn't even pray to ask God to help me. I was challenged to the core of my being!

At the end of a particularly difficult day, I found myself alone in my dorm room, crying out to God for help. I didn't want to repudiate my studies in philosophy and theology. It had enlivened my intellectual life in many exciting ways. I didn't want to go back to my uncritical way of thinking. I had found something that had set me free. I had learned to be analytical, logical, and even creative! I was very excited intellectually. But my faith felt so threatened that I thought I might have to give up such thinking or I might lose my faith altogether.

Without making a conscious decision to pray, I began talking to God (which had been very natural for me to do through the years). And my prayer went something like this: "God, I don't know how to talk with you. I don't even know if I should be talking to you. Perhaps you're the ground of my being; perhaps you're being itself. I don't know . . . Maybe it's only words I'm saying to myself. Maybe all prayers are merely words. I don't know . . . God, are you listening? How do I know you are? . . . If you're not a personal being, how can I pray to you? If I think of you as a personal being, am I just creating you in my image? I don't know . . . God, I need your help. I don't want to give up my faith; but I don't want to give up my thinking either." Then I was silent for a long time. I thought; I anguished; I cried; over and over again. I didn't know what to do. I didn't want to give up my trust relationship with God. But, how could I trust a God I couldn't comprehend? And then – slowly and dimly – a thought began to emerge in my consciousness: perhaps I didn't have to choose between my relationship with God and my intellectual pursuits. I began praying again: "God, there's so much I don't understand. But I'm going to trust you, regardless of the questions that come to mind. I'm not sure if you're a personal being, or the ground of my being, or being itself. But I'm going to trust you, regardless."

It's now decades later. I'm still thinking – more analytically than ever! And I'm still trusting – more deeply than ever!

ADULTHOOD

A crisis of faith and tragedy – struggling with truths #2 and #3

It happened on a Friday evening – many years later. I had just arrived home. Tears were already rolling down my cheeks as I opened the door. There stood my wife, Naomi, looking as distraught as I've ever seen her. We embraced immediately and sobbed in each other's arms.

I didn't want to let go, but I became aware of other people in the room. First I saw my pastor, Phil. We hugged as we cried. Then I saw my assistant from work, Sally, who is Phil's wife. We also hugged as we cried. Then the doorbell rang and there stood my supervisor from work, Neal, the president of the seminary. We also embraced with tears flowing freely.

I don't remember any spoken words except for those that Naomi and I shared as we recounted what we had heard. There had been a series of phone calls. The first one had come to Naomi at home. The message was that our daughter Bonnie had been hit by a vehicle and had been taken to the hospital. Details were unknown.

The message was immediately relayed to me in my office. It was a little after 4:30 p.m. The office was officially closed. I was reviewing words of tribute that I had written for a faculty colleague who was soon to retire and was being honored that evening. As I hung up the phone I went straight to the president's office to let him know that he might need to pinch-hit for me. I gave him a copy of what I had prepared.

As he was reviewing the text, his phone rang. He indicated Naomi was on the line and handed the receiver to me. I listened very intently as I heard her tell me she had just received another call from a family member in Indianapolis. "They've done all they can," she said, "but there doesn't seem to be any hope." I asked questions. Naomi answered as best she could, but she had been given very few details. Then she added, "I think they said they're going to try to keep her alive until tomorrow." My heart sank. I stopped breathing momentarily, and then exploded uncontrollably in tears! I'll never forget that moment! "Then she's really dying," I said to Naomi. "Uh huh," I heard in response.

I hurriedly left my tribute with Neal and asked him to present it on my behalf, but not to indicate what had happened. I didn't want to spoil the evening for my faculty colleagues who were being recognized for their illustrious careers.

It was the details that we had heard in those phone calls that Naomi and I were now sharing with Phil, Sally, and Neal. It became clear to all of us – rather quickly – that Naomi and I needed to leave right away for Indianapolis, a trip of 210 miles.

The five of us decided to join together in prayer. We stood, formed a circle and held hands. And, as we were doing this, some words came out of my mouth without any forethought at all. I heard myself saying, "**Whatever happens, we're going to trust God**."

I don't remember any other words that were spoken in that circle. Phil, Sally, and Neal probably said some thoughtful things. They always do. Each of them probably prayed a meaningful prayer, but all I remember is that they were there. They had come right away. They had shown that they cared. They had joined with us in our excruciating pain.

I kept saying the words to myself over and over again, "Whatever happens, we're going to trust God." They were words springing up from the core of my being. They were comforting. They were strengthening. They were energizing. They served like an anchor to a boat caught in a raging storm.

The ride from Evanston to Indianapolis was very difficult, intellectually and emotionally. The Friday evening traffic through Chicago was incredible. The usual trip of four hours took more than five hours that night. En route we made frequent calls to the hospital from our car. We began to put some pieces together. A city bus had struck Bonnie as she was crossing the street in downtown Indianapolis on her way home from work. She had lost consciousness immediately upon impact, had been taken to the hospital, had undergone surgery to explore the extent of injury to her head, had been diagnosed as unable to survive, and was being kept alive by numerous procedures, devices, and medications until we could get there, and until arrangements could be made for her organs to be donated and transplanted.

Bonnie was such a beloved daughter! She had been an excellent student with nearly a straight A record through high school, had been an Honor Scholar all four years at DePauw University, had gone to law school at Indiana University, and had passed the bar exam in Indiana a semester before she graduated. Even more important, Bonnie had been a faithful and vibrant follower of Jesus Christ – one who believed her faith needed to be integrated with her intellectual pursuits as well as her response to the needs of others.

Remembering who Bonnie was, and all the promise she embodied, made the trip to Indianapolis so indescribably painful. And what intensified the pain even further, was the realization that she would likely be pronounced dead the next day, May 11th, my birthday. I sobbed so heavily as I realized this that I couldn't utter a word. At times it was very difficult to see the road through my tears. And, as if this were not enough, Naomi realized that Bonnie's death would come on Saturday, the eve of Mother's Day!

The details of the next 24 hours would take too long to describe in a postscript such as this. So much happened. So many people were involved. So much pain was felt.

After staying up all night and the entire next day, we concurred with the medical staff and joined them in pronouncing Bonnie dead at 6:15 p.m. Her husband and other family members joined Naomi and me in a large circle around her bed, surrendered her life to God, and prayed for the medical teams that would remove her organs and transplant them into others unknown to us.

Throughout those incredibly difficult hours I found myself still trusting God in the midst of my pain. I hurt so deeply, yet I trusted God as deeply as I hurt. And, though I didn't expect it, my experience of intertwining the two became indescribably profound. Nothing was going to destroy my trust in God, not even the death of my beloved daughter!

Waking up in a strange hotel room on Mother's Day, Naomi and I could scarcely believe we would never see Bonnie alive again. The day before seemed like a dream, yes, a horrible nightmare! Yet we knew Bonnie was dead. Even though it was hard to believe, it was true. Even though it didn't seem real, it was!

So much more happened on that Sunday as calls/flowers/visitors arrived; on that Monday when funeral arrangements had to be made; on that Tuesday evening when hundreds and hundreds of people came to share in our grief; on that Wednesday afternoon when several hundred more came to attend the funeral service at Meridian Street

United Methodist Church, where her casket stood at the communion rail, the very location where she had been married ten months earlier.

Much more happened in the weeks and months that followed. Yet, through it all, I didn't find myself feeling anger toward God. I was angry with the driver for turning the bus into a pedestrian walkway without paying attention and hitting Bonnie very forcefully as she crossed the street with the right of way on a green light; but I worked through that anger.

As the summer went on I found myself wondering if I was denying my anger toward God. I thought about it over and over, as intentionally and honestly as I could. Was my repetition of the phrase, "Whatever happens, we're going to trust God," a way of not dealing with the harshness of what had happened? I thought about it very earnestly.

At the same time, I knew I'd faced harshness many times in my life – directly, candidly, and in full view. I had learned that, for me, it made more sense to deal with reality just the way it was! Perhaps that's why Naomi and I went to the accident scene before we returned to Evanston, and stood at the edge of the street, with tears streaming down our faces, as we watched one bus after another enter the pedestrian walkway precisely where Bonnie had been killed. We wanted to face the stark reality of what had happened.

As the summer drew to a close, I began to realize – through my reflecting and praying – that something else had happened in my life years before. It was nearly twenty years earlier that my other daughter, Becky, at age 14, had been diagnosed with diplopia (double vision) and papilledema (a swelling of the optic nerve caused by a rise in pressure within the brain). That startling news also came on a Friday afternoon. And, by the following Monday, she was in the hospital for tests. Then, a few days later, she underwent the first of nine major surgeries. The initial one tried to remove a growth that was blocking the fluid from moving through the ventricular system of her brain, but couldn't. A shunt was surgically placed to bypass the blockage. Eight more surgeries that dealt with a number of related problems followed, including a massive subdural hemorrhage on the right side of her head (bleeding between layers of the brain). The threat of death came repeatedly. At one of those times, the doctors indicated they had done all they could and that we should be aware that she might very well die that night. It was so serious that we even began making funeral plans.

Becky was a very attractive person, an excellent student, and a leader in her school, in her youth group, and among her many friends. She was already becoming what her parents – and most parents – would want a teenager to be. And, then, very unexpectedly, her world changed. And so did mine, and Naomi's, and Bonnie's.

It seemed so unfair, so incredibly unfair! Why should Becky have such a blockage in her brain? Why should she have to undergo so many surgeries, so many treatments, and so many setbacks? Why should she have to spend over 140 days in one year in the hospital? Why should she have to be in ICU – week after week after week?

It was during these days of anguish on top of anguish that I began to question God more and more. It was not that I hadn't questioned God before. I certainly had – many times. Yet this time the severity of Becky's situation made my questioning much more intense. It was no longer in abstract philosophical or theological categories. It was no longer being carried out from a distance. It was no longer seen in the lives of other families. It was my daughter, my own flesh and blood!

Naomi and I prayed – very earnestly and very fervently – for Becky. We prayed for her with many others. We also asked others to pray for her, for those of us close to her, and for the medical staff who were working so diligently for her well-being.

Yet one complication after another arose, and Becky seemed to get worse, not better. As a result of a massive subdural hemorrhage, she became paralyzed on her whole left side. She couldn't walk. She couldn't go to the bathroom by herself. She couldn't feed herself. And her future became more frightening every day. Glimpses of sunlight came through once in awhile, but the clouds gathering over her life seemed to be getting darker and darker!

It all came to a climax for me one night after I got home from the hospital. I was sitting up by myself. Naomi had gone to bed. I felt such anguish and pain. At times I was in deep thought. At other times I was sobbing. And in the midst of it all, I found myself talking out loud to

God – in order to stay focused – until it was almost dawn. It was a horrendous night! My tears flowed especially freely as I shared my anger with God, and more significantly, as I shared my anger toward God. I even said to God, "It's so unfair. I'm angry, yes, even angry with you!"

I had been told that God could take it. And that night God did. God accepted my anger. God seemed to say that it was OK to be angry. Yet, I felt guilty for expressing such anger. But God seemed to reassure me that I didn't have to deny what I felt. I could express it and know that God would receive me and my feelings – just the way I was – even if God didn't deserve my anger.

I came to a more profound sense of trust that night than I had ever experienced before. I came to trust God in the midst of my anguish, my pain, and my anger. I came to trust God regardless of what might happen in the future! And little did I fathom – at that time – that Becky would eventually overcome her limitations, would exceed the doctor's highest expectations, and would function with hardly any residual after effects!

In the years that immediately followed my night of anguish, and Becky's remarkable recovery, that sense of trust became even more profound. I came to believe – really believe – that whatever would happen, I would trust God. I internalized this belief. It became a part of who I was!

Little did I know – several years later – while dealing with the shocking news that Bonnie had been struck by a bus and wasn't going to survive, that I would blurt out those words, **"Whatever happens, we're going to trust God."** And little did I realize that, when I wasn't angry with God after Bonnie died, that I wasn't denying my feelings, but was affirming what I had learned many years earlier.

Now I know nothing can or ever will destroy my trust relationship with God. It is at the core of who I am!

LOOKING AHEAD

Now that I've shared some of my experience of these truths, it's time for me to encourage you to think about ways you've also experienced one, two, or all three of them. And then to think about ways you might experience them more fully in the days to come.

Next steps are up to you.

Addendum

BIOGRAPHICAL INFORMATION
ADOLF HANSEN

CURRENT

Theologian in Residence, St. Luke's United Methodist Church, Indianapolis, Indiana

Consultant to Churches and Theological Schools, Hansen Consulting, Fishers, Indiana

Senior Scholar and Vice President Emeritus, Garrett-Evangelical Theological Seminary, Evanston, Illinois

Ordained Elder, Indiana Conference of the United Methodist Church

Certified Fellow in Thanatology, Association for Death Education and Counseling

Author of *Responding to Loss: A Resource for Caregivers*. Death, Value, and Meaning Series. Baywood, 2004 (0-89503-301-1)

Coordinating Editor of *Tuesday Mornings with the Dads: Stories by Fathers Who Have Lost a Son or a Daughter*. Inkwater, 2009 (978-1-59299-434-2)

Member, Board of Trustees, University of Indianapolis, Indianapolis, Indiana

FORMER

Graduate of Taylor University (BA), New York Theological Seminary (MDiv and STM), and Northwestern University (PhD)

Professor and Chair, Department of Philosophy and Religion, University of Indianapolis, Indianapolis, Indiana

Adjunct Professor, Indiana University School of Medicine, Indianapolis, Indiana

Director, North Central Jurisdictional Course of Study School, Evanston, Illinois

Adjunct Professor, New York Theological Seminary, New York, New York

Pastor, Simpson United Methodist Church, Fort Wayne, Indiana, and Meridian Street United Methodist Church, Indianapolis, Indiana